RIMO

RIMO

Mountain on the Silk Road

PETER HILLARY

Hodder & Stoughton
LONDON SYDNEY AUCKLAND TORONTO

British Library Cataloguing in Publication Data

Hillary, Peter
   Rimo.
   1. Asia. Karakoram Range. Visitors'
   guides
   I. Title
   915.4'6

   ISBN 0-340-40539-2

First published 1988

Published by Hodder and Stoughton,
a division of Hodder and Stoughton Ltd,
Mill Road, Dunton Green, Sevenoaks, Kent TN13 2YE
Editorial Office: 47 Bedford Square, London WC1B 3DP

Photoset by Rowland Phototypesetting Ltd,
Bury St Edmunds, Suffolk

Printed in Great Britain by St Edmundsbury Press Ltd,
Bury St Edmunds, Suffolk

To Ann

Contents

PART ONE – ALONG THE SILK ROAD
1 Enthusiasm Is Infectious   13
2 Leh's Delays   18
   31 July–14 August
3 Crossing the Saser La   34
   15–19 August
4 Waiting For Wangchuk   48
   20–24 August
5 The Gates of Hell   59
   25–27 August
6 Across the Depsang Plains   68
   27–30 August

PART TWO – THE MOUNTAIN
7 Selecting a Line   87
   31 August–4 September
8 Bad Weather Blues   98
   4–15 September
9 To the South-East Ridge   116
   16–24 September
10 So Close and Yet So Far   132
   25 September – 5 October

PART THREE – DESCENT
11 A Difficult Journey
   6–30 October   149

   Epilogue   175

Acknowledgments

Without sponsors and supporters few trips would ever get off the ground, let alone reach deep into mysterious places and climb high on magnificent mountaineering objectives.

We are especially indebted to Grindlay's Bank for their crucial support and enthusiasm.

And we should also like to say thank you to the following: the Government of India Tourist Office; Air India; R. Gunz Photographic Ltd for Olympus cameras; Paddy Pallin for outdoor gear; Karrimor for packs and clothing; Rolex; Kodak, New Zealand; Arthur Ellis & Co. for Fairydown clothing and sleeping bags; Outdoor Survival, Australia; Sears Roebuck & Co.; American Recreation Products; Mocom Computers.

The main photograph of the cave etchings above the Umlung Nala and the full page view up the South-East Ridge are reproduced by permission of Terry and Brett Ryan. The photography of the ponies negotiating the gorge beyond Murgo; the figures dwarfed by the Depsang Plains; the avalanche above the South Rimo Glacier; and the avalanche below the Khardung La are reproduced by permission of Roderick Mackenzie. All other photographs are by Peter Hillary.

spike milligan

Monkenhurst,
15 The Crescent,
Hadley Common,
HERTS.

21st March, 1986 -

David Read Esq.,
429 Willarong Road,
Caringbah 2229,
Sydney,
N.S.W.
AUSTRALIA

Dear Dave,

Your letter came from out of the blue, or brown or grey or whatever the current colour is. Yes, but the choice of a man who suffers from vertigo to be a Patron is like asking Hitler to run a synagogue. However, if you insist on climbing Mount Rimo, O.K. I will be a Patron, providing you don't fall off, that's when I draw the line. Good luck with your insanity, it's better than most I have read about.

Warm regards,

Spike Milligan.
Poet of Woy Woy.

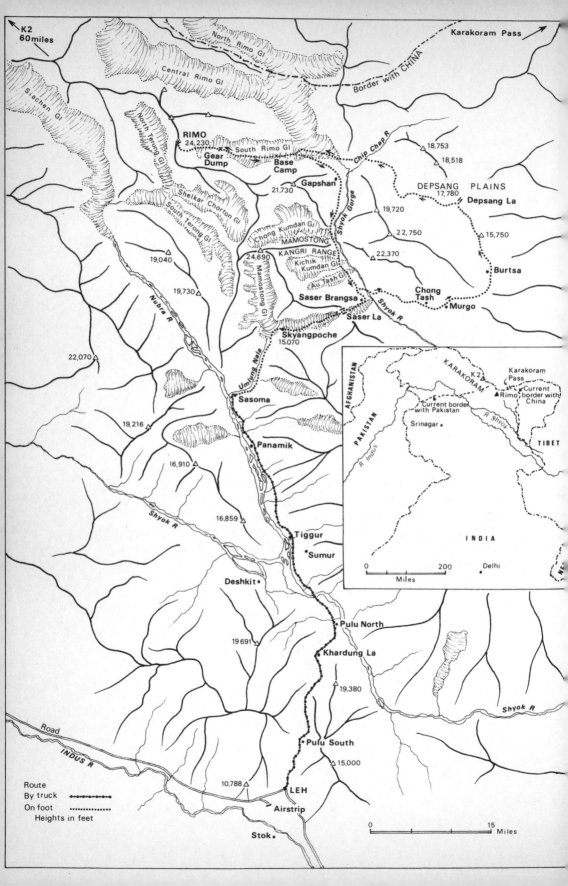

K2
60 miles

North Rimo Gl

Central Rimo Gl

Karakoram Pass

Border with CHINA

Siachen Gl

North Terong Gl

RIMO
24,230

South Rimo Gl

Gear
Dump

Base
Camp

Chip Chap R

△ 18,753

△ 18,518

DEPSANG PLAINS

17,780

Depsang La

Shelkar Chorton Gl

Gapshan

21,730

19,720

△ 22,750

△ 15,750

South Terong Gl

Chong Kumdan Gl

MAMOSTONG

KANGRI RANGE

24,690

Kichik
Kumdan Gl

22,370

Chong
Tash

Burtsa

△ 19,040

Au Tash Gl

Mamostong Gl

Saser Brangsa

Shyok R

Murgo

△ 19,730

Saser La

Nubra R

△ 22,070

Umlung Nala

Skyangpoche
15,070

Sasoma

△ 19,216

Panamik

△ 16,910

△ 16,859

Shyok R

Tiggur

Sumur

Deshkit

AFGHANISTAN

PAKISTAN

KARAKORAM

K2

Karakoram
Pass

Current
border with
China

Rimo

Current border
with Pakistan

Srinagar

R Shyok

R Indus

TIBET

INDIA

0   200
Miles

Delhi

Pulu North

19 691 △

Khardung La

△ 19,380

Shyok R

Road

Pulu South

INDUS R

△ 15,000

10.788 △

LEH

Airstrip

Stok

Route
By truck
On foot
Heights in feet

0   15
Miles

PART ONE

ALONG THE SILK ROAD

1

Enthusiasm Is Infectious

I had to get away from him. I edged past two heavily tattooed fellows who slurped their beers and periodically produced unintelligible utterances from their intensely antipodean larynxes. So far so good.

My shoes were sticking to the beer-drenched carpet and the deafening bashing of the rock-'n'-roll band meant I could only tell that Roddy was talking by the movements of his face and lips. Suddenly, they all laughed and I knew that Mackenzie must be on form. We stood in an unruly huddle in that throbbing Melbourne pub trying to hear each other as we downed our beers and I tried to be inconspicuous. To no avail. Peering over Roddy's shoulder was the man I was avoiding. He had small keen eyes, a large hooked nose and a jutting beard that extrapolated the known dimensions of his chin from here to infinity.

I had seen this look before. The man had spent too much time at high altitude and he had all the most morbid symptoms. A succession of hilarious anecdotes, none of which could possibly be true and, what's worse, as many plans for more preposterous adventures. His intensities reached a crescendo when he spoke of an unknown peak high in the Eastern Karakoram mountains.

'Rimo,' he said.

'What? I can't hear you,' I shouted in the raging din of the bar.

'Reeeemmo!' he roared, sending a shower of foaming saliva across the congregation of friends.

'More beer, anyone?'

'Hell, yeh!'

But not even this diversion quelled this Terry Ryan fellow's enthusiasm for 'Reeemo'.

'We'll be the first foreigners across the Depsang Plains in forty years! The last bloke was Eric Shipton in 1947 when he was on his way to Kashgar in China.' He made a rare pause. 'Did you know the whole area is a mountain desert? There are double-humped camels everywhere . . .'

How could anyone go on an expedition to a remote, desolate, mountainous patch of earth in Central Asia with a man who carried on as this one did? . . . and as for double-humped camels, Freud would have seized upon them as indubitable proof for some of his more sordid hypotheses.

'Where are you from, Terry?'

'I'm from Adelaide, mate.' However, it transpired that Adelaide was a thing of the past as Terry had spent the past eight years in a small village in the Himalaya.

'Bit of an Asiaphile are ya, mate?'

'The climbing is fantastic around Manali,' Terry Ryan continued undeterred, 'and the skiing is incredible. We get runs of five, six, seven thousand vertical feet . . .'

Enthusiasm is infectious. If you can't escape it, you succumb to it – like 'flu. We all met up to do this at Hillside, Roddy Mackenzie's family farm in the Western Districts of the State of Victoria.

I arrived in mid-afternoon. It was very hot and the only things that moved were great squadrons of lazy flies that homed in to form a halo round me and the dust-covered four-wheel drive inside which I sat wiping sweat from my brow.

A shot rang out and then another. I looked out in the direction of the shots. Roddy came swaggering round the corner of the old white weatherboard homestead. Consistent with his philosophy that farm apparel should be rugged, dispensable and, principally, old, his shoes, a pair of expedition issue from a previous mountaineering adventure, had self destructed to the point where he was having difficulty containing his toes. The green cotton trousers were now little more than shredded canvas with a facility for stuffing hands into pockets. Indeed, the uninformed observer would have assumed they were a form of grass skirt, a touching memento from one of Roddy Mackenzie's many exploits. But it was the shirt that had delivered the most outstanding value, as he had worn it since the third form at school. Roddy is a big man. Only two buttons were capable of sustaining the pressure put upon them, with the result that this garment was also well-ventilated. Six feet above this splendidly personalised outfit was the affable Mackenzie smile, alert eyes and an extraordinary mop of tightly curled golden fleece.

Not long after I arrived, Brett Ryan's decrepit old car drew up. Once switched off, the vehicle faltered with a case of pre-ignition which was amply matched by a loud burp from the man with the large hooked nose and the rivetting eyes. He pushed open the door, ejecting himself into an upright position with his right hand proffered towards me and his left grasping a short brown bottle of beer. As he did so there was a clattering sound from within the car as half a dozen empties repositioned themselves on the floor.

'Gidday, mate. How ya goin'? Bloody hot, ain't it?'

'Hi. Well. And yes,' I replied.

It was Terry Ryan again.

Terry's scrawny physique masks considerable strength and agility, while his excellent eye and hand co-ordination mark him as a passionate cricketer and a man who has rarely, if ever, been known to lose a drop of Cooper's Ale between bottle and mouth. He is a most engaging person, a true Aussie whose conversation is a compendium of new and archaic Australian terminologies – 'Gidday' on arrival, 'Ooroo' on departure, and the whole gamut in between.

Roddy suggested we grab a few beers and go for a drive on the farm. It was unanimously agreed. A good omen, I thought. And soon we were parked on a neighbouring high point, hands wrapped round stubbies, gazing out over grazing land, eucalyptus forest and ancient round-topped hills. By contrast, we were planning a journey to a geography endowed with youth, with dramatic ridge-lines and eroding flanks.

We wandered off along the undulating ridge and as we walked I chatted with Brett, keen to hear his thoughts on our new venture. He is characteristically a quiet fellow who listens more than he speaks. Neatly built, strong and agile, like his older brother Terry, he sports a mid-face prominence that demands attention and he is very dress-conscious. Fashionable clothing was so important to Brett that he wore designer jeans during the trek to Rimo Base Camp. He had been a yachtsman before he turned to climbing, enjoying extended voyages in a vessel he described as a tub and preferring to go it alone.

The forthcoming expedition to Rimo had begun as the brainchild of the Ryan brothers. Brett and Terry had met up with Rajiv Sharma in Manali as long ago as October 1984. Rajiv had just come back from climbing Mamostong in the Eastern Karakoram at a time when this whole appetite-whetting region was about to be opened up to foreigners. The minute that happened the climbing applications would be flooding in, so Brett and Terry, encouraged by Rajiv, got out the maps and photographs. The Siachen area seemed too close to the firing line with Pakistan and further north, closer to the Chinese border, would probably be equally fraught. But they spotted a couple of 23,000-feet (7000-metre) peaks with good climbing and relatively easy access to the north of

Mamostong and applied for these. In due course the Indian Mountaineering Foundation contacted them to say that those mountains were not available, but Rimo was.

Rimo, at 24,230 feet (7385 metres), was still unclimbed. The last expedition, in 1985, a joint British and Bombay Climbers' Club venture, had reached the summit of Rimo III (23,037 feet/7233 metres) but failed on the main summit. It seemed the ideal peak. A bit close to China perhaps, with the border only a few miles off, but that border was reasonably stable, and the immediate attraction would be the walk in along the Silk Road, the great international trade route used by merchants and armies over the centuries, which would lead us in a great arc across the famous Saser La and up over the remote Depsang Plains.

2

Leh's Delays
31 July – 14 August

We reached Leh, the capital of Ladakh, on 31 July 1986. To get to this point had taken months of frenzied correspondence between India, various corners of Australia, New Zealand and the United States, and the expedition had expanded from four men on a mount to a mob of around thirty, if one counted every last cookboy. Frankly, after a bit I gave up counting.

Part of the plan was also to raft down the Shyok River after we had climbed Rimo, as an exhilarating finalé to the expedition. It would be the highest river ever rafted. Jack Morrison was in charge of the logistics of the raft trip and would join us at Base Camp towards the end of our climb. He operated a raft trip company in the United States and took clients to wild water all over the world. It was on one of these journeys in Nepal that he had met Terry. We originally intended to take along a professional film-maker, but with all the inevitable unforeseen calls on our already overstretched budget, we soon saw this was a luxury we could not afford and resorted to Do-It-Yourself. The chief burden of the filming would fall on me, Brett Ryan and Dave Read, all of whom had some film experience, although we suffered a budget-decreed shortage of film equipment.

Roddy and I worked full time for three months on expedition sponsorship and finally secured support from

Grindlay's Bank of India. It was their last-minute support that kept us in business. I was sorry for their sake that we weren't able to begin repaying them by indulging in a high-profile media send-off from New Delhi. But the authorities categorically vetoed any publicity until the expedition was over because of the high-security area into which we should be travelling. So Grindlay's had to grin and bear it, which they did with good grace, as we slunk out of town at 3.30 in the morning, if one can slink with a couple of tonnes of kitbags, packs, cardboard boxes, plastic barrels, sacks, tins and skis.

There were six of us foreign climbers, the original party of four completed by Dave Read and Skip Horner. Dave was a friend whom I had met in 1982 at Everest Base Camp when he was with the Canadian Everest Expedition and I was climbing Lhotse. He came from Yorkshire and his rather lyrical accent and light humour easily endeared him to his team-mates. From Canada he had moved to Australia, where he married Renée, a tanned, blonde-haired Sydneysider, and quickly took up the national pastime of barbecues, beer, and wearing shorts. Skip became involved with the adventure through Jack Morrison. He was an expert raftsman and a good climber which made him ideal for the varied plans we had for the expedition. Although no one from the Australian end had met Skip face to face, we talked to him on the telephone regularly and he worked unstintingly in America organising equipment for our journey. We were also taking along two trekkers who would accompany us to the foot of Mount Rimo itself. Renée, Dave's wife, was a nurse and musician and she organised the medical kit for the expedition and administered medications as they were needed. Miriam Mott was a friend of Terry's: a banker by trade, she had met Terry on a Himalayan trek he was leading some years before.

The first thing we did once we had disembarked from our Air India jumbo jet in New Delhi was to contact the Indian

Mountaineering Foundation and meet our Indian counter-
parts for the expedition. Commander Jogindar Singh, the
Vice-President of the Indian Mountaineering Foundation,
had been instrumental in gaining the various permissions
we needed and in selecting the Indian members. He was
someone most of us knew well already and so he began the
introductions.

The rules stipulated that we had an Indian leader if we
wanted to venture beyond the Inner Line and this was
forty-five-year-old Colonel Prem Chand, a serving army officer who had climbed Kangchenjunga on an Indian Army
expedition. He was director of the Manali Mountaineering
Institute and had a wealth of expedition experience behind
him. Prem's team included two of India's strongest mountaineers, Rajiv Sharma and Magan Bissa. Both had been
on several major expeditions: Rajiv worked at the Manali
Mountaineering Institute as an instructor, and the serious
and heavily-bearded Magan divided his time between his
homeland in the Rajastani deserts and the mountains,
his most recent trip being the 1985 Indian Army Everest
Expedition where he had been quite badly injured.

There was also the amiable Errol d'Souza who was studying
for his Ph.D. at Nehru University in New Delhi, J. P. Singh,
an engineer, with his flourishing beard and broad turban,
and Shashank who worked for a prominent travel company
in Delhi. They all seemed very ambitious and exuded tremen-
dous enthusiasm for what lay ahead.

The flight was magnificent. The Himalaya passed beneath
our seats and within an hour and a half the pilot was guiding
the jet on to the ground at Leh. As the aircraft came to a halt,
the first thing I noticed was the largest helicopter I have ever
seen. It was parked alongside our 737 jet and was much
the same size! However this technological oddity drew our
attention for only a short time as we looked around at the
extraordinary landscape into which we had descended.
Moonscapes, void of vegetation, rose above us to craggy

skylines while the green patchwork of the irrigated fields of Leh nestled in the valley north of the airfield. The impact was magnified by the clarity of the thin air and our breathlessness at an altitude of 11,000 feet (3350 metres).

In a convoy of decrepit jeeps we motored up the road to Leh and the Hotel Mandala, our Leh headquarters, which we had scheduled for a two-day stay that turned into a fourteen-day epic.

'There could be some problems with our ponies because of the water in the river. And when you are on a long caravan like ours there can be trouble,' Prem warned.

'When you've got seventy-five ponies there's bound to be some problems,' Terry agreed.

'It's all part of the game,' said Jogindar who had accompanied us from Delhi, but would not be coming beyond Leh with us.

It was important to start with enough ponies because where we were going there would be no chance of picking up replacements.

'Once we leave Sasoma at the road-head we will have to be totally self-contained,' Prem told us. But you could tell he liked the idea of it all and looked forward to the adventure.

'With such a large trip it's not surprising that we've had some upsets with the authorities,' Terry went on, reminding us we still had to sort out our trekking route with the army.

'These are the communication problems between the army authorities and the civil,' answered Prem airily. 'And sometimes what happens is the civil gives you a vague clearance that allows you to climb a particular mountain, like in our case Rimo, whereas army people, through their channels, get given a specific route. They have a route for us which runs beyond Saser Brangsa, up the Shyok River.'

'Which happens to be ten feet underwater at the moment,' I added.

'Yeh!' We all chuckled.

Prem continued. 'Obviously we can't go on . . .'

'That's unless we have brought snorkels,' Terry quipped.

'. . . because of the water,' Prem said. 'These are normal problems with an expedition before departure.'

'It will be sorted out,' Jogindar assured us. 'It will be sorted out, you don't have to worry.'

Sure enough, on arrival in Leh we were informed that our permission was not valid for the Depsang Plains and the Silk Road and that we were only allowed to proceed up the Shyok Gorge, which is impassable during the summer because of the high water levels. Colonel Prem was also warned that the army would be impounding all our film for security scrutiny at the end of the expediton. We heaved a collective expeditionary sigh and began to negotiate. The area didn't have a good record. Three expeditions had been allowed to visit the Eastern Karakoram that year; the French were prevented from ever reaching their mountain due to being given an access route that was not possible for ponies, and the Americans were shelled repeatedly at their Base Camp in the Siachen by the Pakistanis. We were the third team. Our negotiations with the army in Leh rapidly began to convey the impression that they didn't want us to proceed any further either.

Jogindar returned to New Delhi to iron out the problems and Prem and I talked with him on the telephone every day or so while we waited for a decision. During this time we walked the streets of Leh, filmed the town from a dozen different angles and went rafting on the Indus River for a day. The rapids were easy but enough to draw a little adrenalin and to toss one of our complement overboard. Skip Horner arrived from California to join the expedition and a few days later most of the team, including our liaison officer, accompanied our equipment by truck over the Khardung La to the Nubra Valley and the road-end at Sasoma, leaving Prem, Rajiv, Roddy and me in Leh to pursue the permission for the Silk Road.

The army had deputed Captain Papaliappan V as our liaison officer. When we met him he assured us of two things: that he would accompany us 'throughout the expedition' and that the V in his name had no particular meaning. We decided to settle for PV. Tara Singh joined us in Leh, too. He was a close friend of Colonel Prem and also of Terry. Like Prem he was in his forties. He was from Manali, an experienced expedition-goer, and would assist with our camps lower on the mountain, as well as with cooking for our burgeoning ranks.

One afternoon Roddy and I spoke with an old Ladakhi, Tsering Namgal, using Wangchuk, our expedition sirdar, as an interpreter. He was seventy-three and had been involved in some of the caravans along the Silk Road earlier in the century. He wore the traditional cloak and we all sat together cross-legged on the flat roof of his house.

'He went six or seven times over the high plain with his ponies,' Wangchuk told us after cross-questioning the old man in Ladakhi.

'What goods were they carrying?'

'People from Yarkand brought silk carpets, woollen carpets, felt carpets and special woollen goods not available here. There were also people going on *haj*, that is pilgrims going to Mecca. They took from here Indian spices, such as black pepper and dried ginger, textiles and opium and hashish.'

'What animals did they use on the caravans?'

'Horses, camels and donkeys.'

'Any yaks?'

'No yaks.'

'Did many animals and people perish on the way along the Silk Road?'

'Many animals died on the route because of the very hard conditions on the trail. They had to walk for very long distances without much grazing and they died because of fatigue and because of ill feeling.'

'Was there enough water for them?'

'Apart from the scarcity of grass, there was a scarcity of drinking water, too. This contributed to the death of many animals.'

'What about the people? Did many of them get sick or die on these long trips?'

'Yes, many people died. The reason, he says, is because of the high altitude. And there were very old people on their way to Mecca who sometimes became sick and lost their lives.'

'They must have been determined people to put up with these rigours.'

'Yes, they were highly determined people.'

'How many ponies did they lose during each trip over the Depsang?'

'It is very difficult to say what the average would be. There were instances, such as at the Saser La, when there was very heavy snowfall and all were dead, including animals and men. He admits that the death rate would be very high.'

'How many trips did the traders make each year?'

'They can make just one trip over the pass in a year.'

'Why was that? Didn't the trip only take a month each way?'

'He says they spent some time at home and they spent time selling things. In those days there were no retailers or wholesalers. Any trader would sell the whole lot himself.'

'Did they have trouble with bandits?'

'In the northern plains there were bandits. They were Changpas and Kambas.'

'Did they have any trouble with the Hunzakuts from north of Gilgit?'

'They were more burglars and thieves than highway bandits.'

'The route was so long and arduous the profits must have been immense to make it all worth while.'

'The profit margins were very high, about four or five times their input.'

'Were the traders mainly Ladakhis or Yarkandis?'

'People from Ladakh would not go to Yarkand to trade very often. Leh was the market so they would be sitting here buying and selling things that the traders brought with them.'

'Did any of the caravans go on from Leh to Srinagar?'

'Very few of them went on to Srinagar.'

'How many caravans a year arrived here and what was the average size of a caravan?'

'He says there would be one to two hundred animals in a caravan.'

'So our caravan will be, by comparison, quite a small one?'

'Yes. There would also be some petty traders who would not have so many horses. There would be some who would come with just fifteen to twenty horses. Including these, he says, there would have been three or four hundred groups of traders coming here every year.'

'That's amazing. So while they were on the Silk Road they would have been passing other caravans all the time?'

'There was a peak during August, September and October so they would have seen other caravans every day at this time.'

'So we are going in the old peak season. When did the caravans stop coming through the Karakoram to Leh?'

'He doesn't remember when, but says that they came until they were stopped. That was about 1946.'

I knew there had been three crossings of the Karakoram Pass in 1946 because Eric Shipton had been in one caravan on his way to a second period as British Consul General in Kashgar, and he describes the fears of bandit attacks and the worries about whether or not to set out from Leh in his autobiography, *That Untravelled World*.

Wangchuk added that he thought there had been one caravan in 1947. 'That was the last, and not a soul came after that.'

'So it has been a long time since anyone has used the route

for trading. Tell me, did the traders enjoy the trip over to Yarkand?'

'It was really hard but they had to go. They were pleased to go. They were pretty satisfied when they had the reward, you see. In order to get something they had to lose something, in this case their idle time at home. And the pilgrims would be happy because they were on the *haj*.'

It was curiously satisfying to have been able to make this brief link with a way of life that had forged the history of the area as one of the world's great international trade routes.

The four of us left in Leh spent our days making official appointments to talk to the District Commissioner and the army's GOC, and booking phone calls to Jogindar Singh in New Delhi. One day for a diversion Roddy, Prem, Rajiv and I took a vehicle up to Stok, a village on the other side of the Indus River valley from Leh, walked through the magnificent old palace and monastery and then on through the brilliant green fields on the valley floor with the arid, rock-strewn flanks of the mountains stretching above us. The geology of the area is completely exposed and quite remarkable, with rocks in vivid greens and yellows, mauve and purple, grey, charcoal, white and red, like an abstract canvas that reaches as far as the eye can see. There are stupas and chortens made from rock and mud, whitewashed with a micaceous clay, many partially washed away by the infrequent rain and snow of centuries. Over a small crest I could look across fields protected by sod walls and filled with mustard flowers, while up-valley, beyond the luscious green of the valley floor and the desolate mountain flanks, I could see the protruding snout of a glacier among the distant peaks of the Ladakhi Range.

After two frustrating weeks news came through from Jogindar Singh in Delhi that permission to cross the Depsang Plains had been approved. However, the information had to be transmitted through the labyrinth of military communication channels and at each junction there was the infamous communication priority system. We were sure our important message would rank very poorly. What is more, Prem had sent Rajiv to Sasoma with messages for the team warning that progress was slow, so we now needed to send fresh messages to rekindle their enthusiasm.

For three more days we kicked our heels around Leh. We were waiting to make our regular call to Delhi when a man drew up on a motorcycle to tell us that an army officer had arrived at the Mandala Hotel with a message. Prem and I rushed out into the street. Remembering our telephone booking, I ran back to cancel it while Prem jumped on the back of the motorbike and roared down the road to the Mandala Hotel with me in hot pursuit. This had to be it, either the approval had arrived or it was something more terminal. The motorcycle returned to carry me the last few hundred yards to the hotel, where I dashed inside to see Prem talking with a captain from the Lieutenant-General's office. He had a message from the Commander-in-Chief of the Indian Armed Forces instructing the GOC to allow us to proceed with our expedition and for the outposts along the route to be notified of our impending passage. We were overjoyed! Though it was already nine o'clock in the evening, we opened some bottles of beer and rum and set about organising ourselves for a dawn departure.

It was 5.00 a.m. and most of the stalls in the bazaar were still closed, except for the umbrella stall where I felt compelled to purchase one black umbrella, traditionally known to Himalayan travellers everywhere as the most indispensable tool for an approach march.

Colonel Prem's presence ensured we passed the police checkpost without a hitch and drove on up the impressive zigzags of the barren mountainside behind Leh to Pulu South. Here there was another checkpost, this time a military one, which we again passed through easily and continued on up the increasingly dramatic and, at times, alarming mountain road to the Khardung La. This road is an engineering feat, though to call it a road is misleading as it was really a boulder-strewn track just wide enough for a small truck, with huge drops into nothingness on one side and the possibility of large rocks falling on to you from the other: twisted remnants of green army vehicles provided their own warning.

Our driver was a dishevelled character who struggled with the slippery plastic steering wheel as he tried to counter the slack in the steering linkages, the terrible jarring of the road and the unnerving mannerisms of his equally dishevelled vehicle. Periodically, when he loitered too close to the edge of the road on some mystical driving tactic, Roddy would roar a colourful assortment of observations. Throughout all of this Prem stared stoically ahead as if in a dream.

At the Khardung La we visited the little temple and looked north to the grand white shapes of the Saser Kangri and Mamostong mountain ranges before dropping down on an almost interminable descent of plunging zigzags. The road surface was a roughly assorted selection of small boulders which gave me a better understanding of the transition involved for an egg in becoming an omelette. The jeep would bounce around, falter on the crests of these veritable road ranges and then plummet into the tyre-gobbling grotto on the far side.

We had to stop frequently to lash down the equipment, and five times for breakdowns, principally due to a lengthy history of the most economical form of jeep maintenance schedule: none whatsoever. A leak in the petrol pump was temporarily repaired by our enterprising driver by encasing the faulty apparatus in a damp sod of mud and grass wrapped in hessian and generously doused with water. Remarkably it seemed to do the job. The terrain through which we passed was magnificent but difficult to appreciate while constantly reassessing our escape plans in case the decrepit jeep decide to commit harikari.

A hundred and thirty miles from Leh we stopped at a telephone relay station on the roadside where our driver bought petrol from a soldier manning the station. The whole transaction was illegal as the fuel was army property and having it conducted brazenly beneath his nose annoyed Colonel Prem.

He asked the soldier to make us tea, at which the man, obviously a past-master in private enterprise, replied truculently that we would have to pay for it. The Colonel Sahib was so incensed by this lack of hospitality and courtesy that he proceeded to give the squaddie a verbal dressing-down in which he intimated that he was a full colonel, an ex-officer of the Ladakh Scouts and had served in the area himself for two years. The soldier was transformed from his previously disagreeable self into an obsequiously anxious human being – a man concerned about his future in the Indian Army.

'In a few minutes we shall have some tea,' announced Prem, whose good humour had returned.

When we made our departure from the telephone relay station, we left behind a rather forlorn and constantly saluting soldier in a cloud of dust by the roadside.

The lower part of the valley became much broader with vast alluvial plains into which the rivers had cut deep gorges. On the precarious alluvial ledges we came upon the bright green patchwork of fields and small villages. Sometimes there were houses standing out on ledges by themselves with narrow irrigation canals cutting across the mountainsides, taking icy water from upstream to these remote platforms. Above reached the rugged, crumbling mountains of the Ladakh range. There is very little vegetation, so the great screes and tallus slopes lie bare. Up-valley they were black, magenta and gold and above the village yellow and grey with caps of snow upon their peaks. We were at about 14,000 feet and yet the temperature was very pleasant, particularly when one was in the sun; distinctly shorts and T-shirt weather. However, as we came over the Khardung La I noticed that many of the streams and seepages had frozen overnight.

The people here are Mongolian in appearance, similar to the Tibetans and Sherpas, predominantly Buddhist, although there are some Muslims among them. Their houses are flat-roofed adobe boxes, cream or pale grey. Surrounding them would be a few rather moribund willows and poplars and, beyond that, desolation.

The jeep moved at a faltering speed along a road ledge that traversed broad mountainsides to descend to the cold grey waters of a major river. This was the serpentine Shyok flowing down its braided bed, a vast flat alluvial valley floor hemmed in by massive steep walls and peaks on either side; typical post-glacial geography, youthful geology and, best of all, wonderful mountain scenery. It was an exciting moment as this was the river that we planned to raft and, in fact, this was the point where we meant to finish. There was lots of water in the river which we hoped would last until we had finished with our climb of Rimo.

The road dropped down to the river and followed a few rather precarious ledges cut into the alluvial banks. It then led out across the wide river flats to a bridge, an anachronistic steel-grey structure in the middle of nowhere, that would take us across to the Nubra Valley side of the river. We stopped briefly to eat some lunch at this junction of the ways. On the south side of the Shyok River I could see the village of Deshkit, a green patch of trees and fields beneath a tall dark mountainside. The road continued down-valley a short distance before turning north into the Nubra Valley.

We drove up the Nubra Valley for mile after mile. Like the Shyok Valley, it is broad, flat and desolate, the aridity broken briefly by the concentrated effect of irrigation around the little villages of Sumor and Tiggur and, later in the afternoon, at Panamik. As the jeep bounced along the rock and sand path it lifted clouds of dust which coated the vehicle and ourselves with a pale-coloured micaceous powder. Roddy, lying in the back of the jeep on top of some of our gear, seemed ideally placed for dust accumulation. He looked as if he had only recently been released from some medieval prison where he had not seen the light of day for at least a decade. His eyelashes had come in for a particularly severe powdering, which Prem and I thought did wonders for his appearance.

It was no surprise to us when the vehicle broke down yet again on one of the many lonely and parched stretches of the Nubra Valley. This time it was a linkage from the gear levers to the gearbox that had gone. Our driver contorted himself under the jeep, to no avail, so he began pounding a hole in the floor pan with a cold chisel which enabled him to poke a piece of wire down to the linkage and hold it in place. This allowed us to drive the last few miles through Panamik and on towards Sasoma.

Among the rock bluffs hundreds of feet above the village of Panamik we could see a huge cavern. There were plenty of stories about it; some said that this was where an ancient tribe had lived and the locals believed it to be an abode of spirits. Just below Panamik on the far side of the river there was another even larger cave, again several hundred feet above the valley floor and its entrance about one hundred feet across. Roddy had read that archaeological fragments of some past civilisation had been discovered here, but we were the wrong side of the river to investigate for ourselves. There were other intriguing sites upon the ledges of the valley walls. High and remote were monasteries with a few slender green poplars, their dark windows looking out over the great expanse of the Nubra. Very often they were so inaccessible that it was difficult to see any evidence of the path to the valley floor. I couldn't help reflecting on the monks whose lives were cloistered by such intensely isolated asceticism.

The Nubra Valley is immense, about three or four miles wide and its overall length in the vicinity of eighty miles. Its surface is relatively flat, interrupted periodically by gentle shingle fans extending from the mouths of deep gorges that have cut their canyons in the valley's flanks. It is on these fans that most of the villages are to be found with their networks of irrigation ditches leading from the mountain streams above, the aridity of the region softened by the late summer colouring of apricot, poplar and willow trees. During the winter months the villages adopt the stark tones of the desert. For desert it surely is; many areas receive only three to four inches of rain a year, so their viability is exclusively due to the glacial melt from the mountains all around.

The villagers build sod walls around their fields of barley, mustard, potatoes and swedes to keep their foraging animals at bay. These include yaks and ponies, mules and donkeys and goats and sheep. On the flat roofs of their houses the villagers lay out the harvested grain and livestock feed to dry in the sun, ready for the long cold winter ahead. Once the feed is dry they pile it up around the edge of the rooftop to form a parapet. The villagers were fascinated by our presence, as most of them had never seen white people before. They came scuttling out of their houses to have a look, smiling and waving at these ghostly, grey-faced beings who emerged from the dust.

After a long day on the road we reached Sasoma where we visited the military camp. This had been one of Prem's responsibilities during his sojourn here as an officer with the Ladakh Scouts a few years before. There was plenty of excitement among the soldiers as they welcomed Prem with beaming grins, long vigorous handshakes and hot cups of tea that tasted like a sweet syrup and were a measure of their esteem for Prem. I was itching to move on, not only to hasten being reunited with the vanguard of the expedition, but also because the army camp was directly in line with a colossal landslide of giant rocks, some of which had already tumbled across the road and right up to the wall of the canteen. Some of the boulders were fifteen feet high and, looking up, I

Ladakhi ladies in the streets of Leh.

A line of chortens at Stak, the village across the Indus from Leh.

Waiting for permission: Prem, Roddy and Peter at the Mandala Hotel, Leh.

The gompa on the ridge above Leh, prayer flags flying in the breeze.

Terry follows the pony caravan down a typical rubble-strewn track.

Ancient cave etchings above the Umlung Nala show a much less arid world and man, with his bow and arrow, in pursuit of game.

A pony picking its way across the raging Umlung Nala.

Skyangpoche, our camp at 15,200 feet.

Unnamed, unclimbed – a superb 23,000-foot granite peak near the Saser La.

The track up the thirty-seven zigzags above Sasoma.

Ponies meandering through the moraines below the Saser La.

Descent from the boneyard of the Saser La.

Rock pinnacles above the Shyok Gorge.

Roddy jumps a swollen tributary of the Shyok, not a place for hesitation.

Scant grazing for our hardworking ponies in the Shyok Valley.

A bleak and ghostly world in the mountains near Saser Brangsa.

Our caravan approaches the Shyok River with the
great Red Wall beyond.

Skip, below the séracs of the Kichik Kumdan Glacier.

The cable-way across the Shyok at Saser Brangsa.

Long practice at lobbing stones to keep ponies on course across a river made the pony wallahs excellent cricket out fielders.

could see that the bluff above was in an alarmingly unstable condition. Living in these barracks must be like living beside a large time bomb.

We drove the last few miles to where we were told the expedition was camped. This would be as far as we could go in our near-to-expiring jeep. The road snaked through the deep cleft in the barren plain created by the explosive exit of the Umlung Nala River from the gorge above and then out across the fan on the far side. Looking up towards a great wall of granite, we could see the characteristic yellow topknot of a North Face dome tent standing up above a sea of boulders – the rest of the expedition. The jeep was thrown abruptly into first gear and we laboured up the slope through a complex boulder garden to a camp of a dozen or so assorted tents and an enthusiastic reunion. We were now a team and after months of hassle and stop-go bureaucracy the expedition really looked as if it was under way.

3

Crossing the Saser La
15 – 19 August

While they waited for Roddy, Prem and me to sort things out in Leh and catch up, the main party had been under virtual tent arrest, confined to camp by the army and the Indo-Tibetan Border Police. So our telegram telling them that all was well and we were on our way caused them to break open the whisky supply in celebration.

'I was thinking of saving you a nip,' Terry confided solicitously, 'but we just couldn't remember if you liked whisky.'

The military had allowed them out in the immediate vicinity and they had been able to raft a section of the Nubra River. Otherwise they had spent their time reading, playing cricket and climbing on the boulders around camp.

During one of their cricket games Terry had hit the ball off among the boulders. Brett sprinted in pursuit while Terry and JP dashed up and down the makeshift pitch accumulating runs until Brett shouted to them to come and look at a remarkable discovery. The boulder above where the ball had come to rest was covered with intricate man-made etchings. It seemed likely that they dated from at least the early Indus Valley civilisation and thus would be about five thousand years old. Mindful of our filming responsibilities, Dave filmed a re-enactment of the discovery before everyone retired for tea.

Roddy, Prem and I sloped off with towels and soap and

flashlights in the evening gloom to wash our dusty bodies in the cold grey waters of the Umlung Nala. It was a shocking experience and was probably responsible for the fact that none of us washed a great deal from that day on. The combination of glacial meltwater and the plummeting temperatures of an evening at ten thousand feet literally took your breath away. I felt as if I could have sung a few bars with the Vienna Boys' Choir.

We rose early the next morning and began dismantling our tent village. All the equipment was packed into twenty-five-kilo loads, each skinny little pony carrying two. Because of the lengthy delays, most of the ponies we had organised had, in the interim, been seconded to the army, leaving us only twenty to carry the essential items along the route to Base Camp. Wangchuk was going to stay behind with the remaining two-thirds of the gear until the ponies taken by the army were returned to Sasoma and able to follow us along the Silk Road to Saser Brangsa, where we would pick up another loop of the Shyok River.

It was a beautiful morning and I felt uplifted by our surroundings. Roddy was more mundanely employed, sitting on a glacial boulder concocting a letter on his portable typewriter. It was to the Ararat District Court to explain why he would not be able to attend the hearing at the end of his one-year good-behaviour bond on the charge of possessing an unlicensed firearm on his farm. He hoped the court would understand that it would be inconvenient for him to do so.

On the polished glacial boulders around camp we found many more examples of the primitive etchings the cricketers had discovered. They depicted a people who were nomadic hunters and had come up these great valleys to follow the huge herds of deer, ibex and antelope. Men with bows and arrows pursued ibex with long gnarled horns and antelope with the more elaborate antlers. I recognised animals that looked like yaks and camels and in some there were men who appeared to be shooting arrows at one another. For us to say that we were the first foreigners in forty years to venture into this part of the world paled to insignificance beside the evidence that surrounded us, for there has been a human presence here for thousands of years. These etchings excited me. In some respects they were an ineffable contrast to ourselves and all our twentieth-century paraphernalia and yet our trekking through this area was not at all different in spirit or style from the journeys made by these ancient people.

Before long we were on our way across the dusty flat to the foot of the awe-inspiring wall of the thirty-seven zigzags. The film group split into two with Dave and his wife Renée remaining behind to get some long shots of our little caravan winding its way up the steep mountain track above. As the morning progressed so the heat rose and after reaching the top of the great rock wall we dropped down the far side into the Umlung Nala and out of sight of the Nubra Valley for what transpired to be two long months: one month longer than we had anticipated and a month that took a great deal of explaining when we got home.

The Umlung Nala was a raging torrent of glacial meltwater. We followed the nala in the extreme heat with huge walls of glowing, golden granite rising three to four thousand feet above us on both sides. Some of it had a polished sheen and other sections were broken by splendid vertical cracks and, here and there, great sheets of rock had exfoliated and formed wonderful chimneys and off-width cracks and towering corners and airy horizontal roofs. Here and there wild roses sprouted from cracks where there were slimy seepages, the blooms standing out among the tones of the desert.

Partway along the gorge we came to a smooth cavity that had been ground into the rock by swift-flowing water. Inside this polished recess were dozens of prehistoric etchings – ibex and antelope again and ancient hunters with their bows firing arrows at the animals. We noticed, however, that large sections of the outer lip had been blasted with explosives by the over-zealous efforts of the Indian Army to improve the track through the gorge.

A little further along this narrow and exposed track we reached the remains of an old army camp in one of the most miserable and narrow sections of the gorge. It had been built, we were told, during the disastrous war with China in 1962. The buildings were dug into the ground and surrounded by sacks of gravel and disused jerry-cans piled up to form solid defensible walls, over which was laid a roof of corrugated iron beneath a thick layer of sand and gravel. They would have been very difficult to see from the air. Most were now collapsed or in the process of becoming so and this legacy of a cruel and unrewarding war conveyed a sense of sadness and futility. I was glad to leave and stroll on along the dusty path.

Beyond the old camp we came to a natural bridge across the Umlung. A huge boulder was jammed across the narrow gorge and the chocolate-milk waters boiled out below. A short distance further on we came to where the path crossed the river. Another boulder had fortuitously become lodged forty feet above a spectacular chasm. This abyss was no more than ten feet wide and its vertical walls were scalloped and glistening. Rising with the deafening roar of the river was a fine spray that settled on the morainic debris above the river and upon us, causing our hair to glisten in the afternoon sun. Not long after I crossed, a pony stumbled on the bridge and, had it not been for the quick reactions of one of the pony wallahs, we would have lost him to the furious currents below, along with two valuable barrels of irreplaceable climbing equipment.

On the far side of the river a steep zigzag trail ascended the crumbling extremity of the valley's alluvial platform. It was still very hot. I perspired heavily and became quite dehydrated. So it was with some relief that I reached the top and was able to move along the barren platform that runs up each side of the valley, the river cutting a deep furrow in the middle. Three hundred yards brought me to a little oasis; a bright green carpet of grass and crops nestled among a maze of ten-foot-high boulders. There were a few irrigated paddocks where barley and mustard grew and two simple stone huts where a family from the Nubra Valley were spending the summer months. It was an ideal place to camp.

We all got on with the pleasant and necessary business of drinking copious quantities of tea. As we chatted, a familiar mop of tangled blond hair appeared from among the granite boulders, a huge pack filled with camera equipment on his back and a rather pathetic specimen of a goat in his arms.

'Where on earth did you get that, Roddy?' I queried.

'I caught him at the old army camp. The poor bastard has been stabbed twice in the neck.' Roddy proceeded to spend much of the evening treating the goat, bandaging its wounds and encouraging it to drink some electrolyte solution. We assumed that some fairly incompetent person had intended to have goat curry, but the goat had had other ideas and, after putting up with being stabbed inefficiently in the neck, had managed to make its escape, avoiding the cooking pot and the seasonings.

PV, our liaison officer, was fitting into the group reasonably well, and seemed to be enjoying the trip, although clearly totally unfamiliar with the practicalities of mountain trekking, for he was a man from the south of India. When the team first arrived in Sasoma he had announced that he could see no reason why we should not take jeeps all the way to Base Camp, despite the 2000-foot granite wall directly above the camp that posed the first obstacle on our trek to Rimo. Another of his choicer pieces of advice was that a helicopter would be a good alternative to the 'jeeps to Base Camp' proposal and that way we could fly directly to 20,000 feet, which he claimed he had done before with no adverse effects other than a slight headache.

I returned to my tent after dinner and lay in my sleeping bag pondering our progress after our first day out from the road-head. It was 16 August and we had been away from home for nearly a month and yet we had only just begun our journey.

It was windy next morning when we left Umlung camping ground, which pleased us all as it kept the temperature down, despite the blue sky and the intense sunshine. We trekked for a few miles up the broad and desolate valley to where it was crossed by a nala draining the Saser Kangri mountains. It was now late morning, so the stream was fast and full with glacial melt which meant wading. We filmed the ponies slipping and sliding with their fifty-kilo loads over the mobile stones of the stream bottom. In single file they crossed the stream and wound their way up the rubble bank on the other side, dust rising in the wind as they reached the top and disappeared from view. We lingered in the sun waiting for the pain in our freezing feet to subside and then followed the caravan up the long valley.

The geology changed as we ascended the valley. Granite spires of golden-brown and grey, with fresh exfoliations the colour of butter, gave way to a region of stratified sedimentary outcrops with elegant veils of tallus sweeping down to the valley floor. Wherever there was water we found a spartan pasture and as we moved up-valley we passed the occasional flock of sheep and goats grazing. But there were no villages, no people, no crops and no substantial vegetation.

At the head of the Umlung Nala we reached the junction of the Mamostong Glacier and a side valley that led to the Saser La and up which our route lay. I paused briefly to look up the Mamostong Glacier to the peaks of the massif including the mighty Mamostong itself, a 25,000-foot (7500-metre) mountain, and only recently climbed. Then turning east, we followed a meandering animal track through some undulating moraine hillocks where we passed a flock of goats tirelessly grazing on the sparse vegetation. Another few hundred yards, and we reached the night's camp at

Skyangpoche where the ponies were being unladen and released for a night of grazing on the alpine stubble.

Since we were now at 15,200 feet the sinking sun was accompanied by a considerable drop in temperature and we all began digging in our packs for our down jackets before settling down to a particularly miserable meal. Our cook, Jonga, had been employed, as Wangchuk later told us, because he was the cheapest available. With rumbling and unsatisfied stomachs we all retreated to our tents. Outside, the sky sparkled with the lights of the Milky Way.

The next day we stayed at Skyangpoche both to assist our acclimatisation and to prevent us from becoming too far separated from Wangchuk and the bulk of our equipment in Sasoma. All the same, when an expedition's progress slows to the pace of a sulking schoolboy, the sluggishness seems to rub off on the participants. Horizontal contemplation of the inside tent roof becomes the order of the day and some sort of lethargy principle takes over to slow down the expedition even more.

After an uninspiring breakfast we attended to various tasks around the camp. Roddy, switching roles from his previous position as good Samaritan to goats, took on the job of butcher of goats, which both surprised and relieved us all, as he is a vegetarian but none of the carnivorous members wanted to do the job. Before I headed up the hillside for some exercise and a look around I went to see how he was getting on. There was blood splattered all over his shirt and smeared across his throat. It was an alarming sight. Had there been a scuffle? I asked.

'Well, as I cut the jugular,' Roddy explained, 'blood gushed everywhere . . .' I didn't stay to hear the rest, and hurried to catch up with some of the others who were climbing up the side of the valley. We scrambled up huge screes with patches of vegetation growing wherever it was stable enough for the plants to survive – yellow buttercups and daisies, edelweiss and in several places we found clumps of alpine poppies, their strong violet colour throwing splashes of wonderful contrast against the scree. Across the valley was an unclimbed 23,000-foot (7000-metre) pyramid-shaped peak with no obvious line of ascent. When we climbed still higher the four main summits of Mamostong rose above the rest like whitecaps at sea, their snowy contoured peaks silhouetted against the azure sky. To the west lay the white crescent of the Saser La hemmed in by crags and more snow peaks. The pass which we should soon be crossing involved extensive glacial travel which, from what I could see, would not be too difficult for us but promised to provide a challenge for our laden ponies.

We were constantly reminded of the fact that this was a war zone. Heavily armed troops accompanying their pony caravans passed by our camp on their way down-valley and a short distance below us was a large military tent, used as a telephone relay station and a trail-side mess for transitting soldiers. The telephone lines were a constant amazement to us as they were draped over rocks, along the tracks and casually slung over streams. Horses trod on them frequently. We were not surprised to hear that the military were often frustrated by communications which ranged, we were told, between the unreliable and the nonexistent. Twice a day helicopters flew overhead en route to the border encampments and we heard the dull drone of transport aircraft high in the sky.

Back at camp Roddy had a magnificent repast awaiting us. Goat soup with chapattis and butter followed by a spiced goat stew with cashews and rice and the last of our green vegetables. Feeling well fed we staggered off to our tents for an afternoon siesta. The warmth of the sun filtered through the nylon so we were able to read and listen to music in the comfort of our solar-heated abodes until a shadow swept across the camp. Looking out, I could see flares of golden light rising from the mountainous western skyline as the sun sank from view. Several people were outside, cameras in hand, capturing the evening splendour on film. When I look back on it, this became a regular evening ritual which signalled the end of the day and a time to socialise before the dark and the biting cold drove us into our tents.

People were congregating around the cook tarpaulin where steam was issuing from large aluminium pots. Everyone kept moving around as they ate, stamping their feet and pulling woollen caps down over their ears. It was ten degrees below zero as we stood outside beneath a canopy of stars and munched our rapidly cooling food. Skip had a good knowledge of the stars and began pointing out many of the constellations. As we gazed at the North Star it occurred to me that it shone directly over our objective, Mount Rimo, and yet ahead of us lay a circuitous route, a veritable dog-leg, in order that our caravan could reach the mountain. Tomorrow we would travel east over the Saser La to the Shyok River again, and then to the Depsang Plains where we would turn north and eventually west towards the South Rimo Glacier. At the glacial snout we planned to establish Base Camp, still about twelve miles from the mountain itself.

At five-thirty in the morning I awoke to a rather blustery and overcast day. A cold front had come through following the high cirrus that glided across yesterday's blue skies. Altostratus sat gloomily overhead, decapitating the summits of the higher peaks and nestling low over the Saser La where there was a deep crimson glow on the underside of the clouds. 'Red sky in the morning, shepherd's warning.'

A hand thrust a large mug of tea into my tent and I braced myself to contemplate the transitional agonies of leaving my cosy bag, packing away the contents of my little nylon home and preparing the loads for the ponies.

We climbed to broad alpine meadows where clumps of gaudy flowers lent a fleeting splash of colour to the braided river flats and the sprawling moraines. As we walked amidst the tinkling bells of the laden ponies I looked up at the peaks that hemmed in the Saser La on both sides. Great buttresses swept up to the summits, some of which were capped with cornices and ice-cliffs. It seemed an extraordinary place for horses to be and yet on we went, further into the glacial wilderness, each of us choosing his own pace. Before long we were spread out along miles of this old Silk Road, a string of coloured glass beads tossed down amongst the rubble.

The trail ascended the dry moraines and we could look down on to the white ice of the glacier and into the brilliant turquoise glacial lakes that abounded near its terminus. All those tales of hardship suffered by caravans over the centuries no longer seemed the exaggerations of legend as the track became littered on all sides with the bleached skeletons of yaks and ponies; there must have been thousands upon thousands of skeletons.

Pausing with Brett, Skip and Roddy to munch a greasy chapatti and peanut butter sandwich in this great boneyard made me consider how the first traders to have established this fearsome route across the Karakoram must have been on an adventure as momentous as the exploration of space seems to us. It is a testimony to the degree of difficulty that the Himalayan barrier represented to the old traders that they chose a route as inhospitable as this one to be their best alternative.

I gazed, mesmerised by my thoughts, across the whiteness of the glacier. Something moved. Looking to the right, a dark object appeared from behind a wall of ice. It grew steadily and to my amazement turned into one of our ponies which was soon followed by another and another. A 'caravan on ice' walked slowly by, like the lost spirits of the skeletons that lay around where we sat and that still inhabited the Silk Road. The pony caravan filed by, gingerly stepping over small crevasses as they went, and disappearing beyond a great pile of glacial detritus.

We bundled up the remains of our lunch and raced off after the spectre that had just drifted up the glacier. So often during the expedition what we saw conjured images of the past and not surprisingly, as many of our experiences were governed by a sense of the timelessness of the land. And where the sky was loud with a passing army helicopter, symbol of twentieth-century power politics, one could imagine instead marauding hordes playing the great game of conquest over the previous centuries.

The trail meandered through the boulder chaos of the lateral moraine and up ahead the ponies clambered back on to the moraine as the glacier began to steepen with deep folds in its surface. We accompanied the ponies as they fought their way over large rocks, their shod hooves often causing sparks to fly into the air. The pony wallahs pushed and shouted and when a lot of encouragement was needed they hurled stones the size of fists at the creatures struggling beneath our fifty-kilo loads. At the top of one tall morainic mound I could see that the route led down to the ice again. It was a steep and loose descent and, as if to reinforce its perilous nature, the rotting carcase of a horse lay jammed among the boulders of a glacial stream at the bottom. One by one the tiring horses negotiated this obstacle, often sliding with all four legs splayed apart, nostrils flared and ears forward, with rocks tumbling around their hooves and the shouts of the pony wallahs in their ears. At the stream they would recoil and jump for the ice on the far side, sending a shower of ice splinters into the air as their hooves bit into the surface. They almost trotted away from the stream and up on to the wide, flat expanse of the Saser La as we gasped in the 17,300-foot air to keep up. The ponies produced plenty of antics as they wove their way around crevasses, jumping the smaller ones and deviating from the pony wallahs' selected route, bringing a chorus of shrill whistles, slaps on the rump and the occasional boot in the rear when they balked at the more terrifying abysses.

The Saser La is a huge place, a vast glacial plain at 17,000 feet (5000 metres) littered with rocks and yet more skulls and skeletons of those who had failed to complete the journey across the pass. We were elated at reaching the top for, with every such crossing, we were moving deeper into the Eastern Karakoram and further along the Silk Road. But it was too cold to linger and it was evident the ponies had no intention of doing so as they headed down the gradually descending glacier that poured like a great freeway towards the Shyok River several thousand feet below. Passing a tiny Hindu shrine, built by the soldiers, with flags cracking in the wind, we followed the convex glacial tongue that pointed ever more steeply towards the narrow gorge below, descending with that new-found vigour that one acquires when gravity is on one's side. Before us was a vista of desolate mountains and huge tallus slides of different hues; one was jet-black streaked with white, others gold and red.

The descent was relentless and I could feel the loss of altitude. To one side of the glacier, upon a moraine, three large furry mastiffs bounded off among the boulders. I pointed this out to Roddy who in turn directed my gaze to the body of a dead horse on which they had been feeding. We speculated on how long the poor beast had been dead and decided that, in an environment as cold and dry as this, it could have been there for as long as two or three years. This possibility made the scene more macabre. Here the limited dignity of decomposition was denied.

The glacier ice gave way to grey moraines and a final terminus that dropped steeply into a side valley draining into the Shyok River. At the upper limit of the meagre vegetation were the squat bunkers and primitive sod barracks of the Saser Brangsa army post. We descended towards a group of soldiers gathered at the upper limit of the camp to be greeted by a most convivial and hospitable major, their commanding officer. He offered us tea, sweet biscuits and spiced pastries while we talked about our expedition and assiduously avoided anything do with the Indian military presence, a topic that we realised was particularly taboo. The major cautioned us not to photograph any military installations, including the camouflaged bunkers that peppered the mountainsides and which I had not noticed until he had been so good as to point them out. We shook him briskly by the hand and made our way down the last thousand feet to the river. There we moved upstream so as to be camped well away from the army, which was their wish, and to minimise the security risk that we, apparently, presented.

I was ecstatic. It was beginning to feel as if we were going to get to Rimo after all! A light drizzle created wonderful rainbows that veiled the ghostly images of these barren, eroded mountains whose colours rivalled those of the rainbow. Shafts of low-angle light flooded into the head of the valley as we traversed a golden hillside. We climbed on to a knoll and ahead glowed a great ochre outcrop, etched, grooved and pinnacled like a cathedral. One million striations crossed its vast face and for every layer I could imagine a million years of geological secrets laid bare. The brilliance of this 6000-foot (1800-metre) high wall was sufficient for me to question whether it was from this that the shafts of sunlight shone, not from above. Its veins of blood red and shields of bronze and gold with flying buttresses of salmon pink beckoned to us with a hypnotic force and we all immediately resolved to explore this part of the valley. The glowing cathedral was topped by a coronet of jagged peaks, while swirling past its base were the cream-grey waters of the Shyok, squeezed in against the ochre wall by the advance of the icefall from the Kichik Kumdan Glacier. The white, residual glacial shapes of the icefall resembled queues of marching penguins.

Our camp was perched on a windy knoll above the river, about a mile below another glacier, the Au Tash, and well positioned near a 'flying fox' cable-way that we would use to cross the river. Already some of our tents were being put up in the fading light of evening and people were making themselves at home here as we planned to stay for a couple of days until Wangchuk arrived with the equipment we had left behind at Sasoma. It was 7.00 p.m. as the last few tents were erected on the rubble-strewn knoll with the occasional bloom ekeing out an existence on the grit. The familiar call went out for tea and dinner, to be met by the equally familiar groans and sighs as each of us summoned the strength necessary to consume a plate of Jonga's abominable cuisine in the chilling windy darkness. I looked at Dave who just shook his head stoically at the pile of congealed rice on his plate.

'I won't tell you what this reminds me of,' he growled.

Just then a soldier arrived from the military camp with a message from PV who seemed to have been waylaid. He said he had been unable to find our camp and had, therefore, and with some reluctance, returned to the army post to spend the night. He would rejoin us in the morning and instructed us not to worry. JP muttered something about hot showers, good food and the company of fellow officers being a contributory factor to his inability to locate our camp, to which we all mumbled agreement. Dave continued to shake his head and stare at the contents of his plate.

4

Waiting for Wangchuk
20 – 24 August

In the night we were all surprised by a storm hurling icy droplets of rain horizontally up the narrow valley. For we had been told that 'the blue cloudless skies of Ladakh' only permitted an annual rainfall of between two to four inches. So after that, whenever the elements were behaving contrary to our wishes, 'the blue cloudless skies of Ladakh' became the phrase bandied about with increasingly desperate sarcasm.

On 20 August however we were greeted by a blustery dry morning, the sun peering through layers of cloud and a sprinkling of new snow on the high peaks. It looked as if it was going to be a beautiful day. Everyone had things to do. I added guy-ropes to most of the tents to secure them against the evening wind and while I went about my task I took great pleasure in the surrounding pale colours of the eroded mountains and the deep Shyok Valley.

There was unanimous approval for sparing the last of the goats we had bought at Skyangpoche from the cooking pot. Grindlay, as we called him, became the expedition mascot and a Grindlay's Bank flag was attached to each of his twisted horns. We planned to take Grindlay to Base Camp and back to Leh at the end of the expedition. He rapidly became one of the camp's personalities and we all became rather fond of him; even his penchant for gnawing on tent guy-lines and people's washing was overlooked.

After lunch the weather deteriorated again as a succession of black storms marched steadily up the valley. By late afternoon they were battering the camp and we feared for our buckling tents. But once the wind and rain had abated they bounced back with reassuring flexibility. By evening the storms had cleared and we all gathered on the crest of the knoll to admire the grandiose vista as the light changed and the remaining clouds dissolved, exposing the rising disc of the moon. As it became darker we could see, using the big 350-mm lens, a glowing red speck which we concluded was Mars, and the bright light of Jupiter with two of its moons clearly visible in orbit around it. We queued like unashamed tourists for use of the lens up on that remote Central Asian knoll, such was our excitement at the clarity of the heavens and our ability to view with our own eyes a planetary neighbour and its orbiting moons.

It was snowing lightly when I awoke next morning and to accompany the meteorological gloom came the news of delays for Wangchuk's caravan. The ponies we had seen at Skyangpoche had failed to reach Sasoma that day and once they did arrive, they took a day off to rest. Consequently, they would not reach Saser Brangsa for at least three days. These delays were disastrous. As the season goes on the summer melt ceases and so the river level drops, leaving the Shyok but a shadow of its former self and unsuitable for our proposed raft descent at the end of the expedition. High up on the mountain we would experience much colder conditions and the effect of the lowering jet stream with its extreme winds. What is more, we would have less overall time for the ascent. We had requested permission to travel within the sensitive Inner Line until 15 October, but had been told we must leave the area by 30 September. This would now almost certainly be insufficient time in which to complete our objectives. We applied for an extension and Prem sent messages through the military radio to prompt it.

On top of this we were beginning to feel increasingly

irritated by the lack of all the desirable commodities we kept discovering were still in Sasoma – like most of our food, the medical kit, spare batteries for our film and sound gear, two sets of stereo speakers, the large mess tent, the rafts, our mountaineering gear and six precious bottles of rum.

Skip, Magan, Terry, Roddy and I decided to reconnoitre the Shyok Gorge and in this we were joined by the major from the army post and two dishevelled soldiers. The major rode along looking as fresh and at ease with the world as only Indian officers can. We set out together but, being on foot ourselves, we soon separated. Passing the dilapidated mechanical structure that masqueraded as a flying-fox cableway across the river, we walked across the broad gravel flats to a gut that cut through the terminal moraines of the Au Tash Glacier and brought us to a recently constructed track leading across the moraines to the ice. We had not seen the major and his soldiers for some time and assumed that they had taken another route or even turned back, so we scrambled down to the ice and the banks of a fast-flowing glacial stream. We leapt and bounded our individual ways across this obstacle, passed below the glacier snout and out on to an interminable alluvial flat that spread before us for miles towards the Kichik Kumdan Glacier and the great Red Wall. We were rapidly reduced to a group of tiny figures moving in a vast wilderness and when I looked back I spotted the correspondingly diminutive forms of the major and his men watching us from the moraine above the glacial stream. There was a sense of satire in our two minuscule groups standing two miles apart and staring at one another, particularly in such an open environment without cover. Our every action was candidly clear and produced the same coyness that one feels in a state of total nudity.

Dust rose around our feet as we plodded across the river plain and as we marched we examined the red cathedral wall that grew before us with every step. It was a complex work of art; stratified and sculpted, with prows and buttresses, deep clefts and gullies dividing the face, rising to spires and pinnacles. While at the northern end, high above us, an obelisk was emblazoned against the blue sky, its summit far broader than its narrow base.

Reaching the Kichik Kumdan Glacier we made our way through the maze of séracs, like an assortment of elegant penguins, and on to a pale rock outcrop that overlooked a slot the river had cut in the bedrock and through which it surged. We sat on one of the glacial, smoothed humps of rock and had our lunch with the sun pouring down upon us. Nearby there was a rock pool of clear water from which we could drink our fill. Up behind the head of the glacier rose a band of unnamed peaks with steep ice-clad rock buttresses dropping into the cwm below. Somewhere beyond these mountains was the Mamostong group but cloud was gathering in the upper glacier and obscured our clear view of what lay beyond.

Jolting ourselves from our siesta we continued up the rocky side of the river beneath the red-bronze face. This led us along the gorge to a cataclysm. The entire river was funnelled to the narrow lip of a fifteen-foot-high fall over which it plunged with a deafening thunder. The full force of the water was directed on to a giant anvil stone that choked the runnel, causing it to shower spray into the air as it deluged past, racing down the twenty-foot-wide gut carved in the solid bedrock at accelerated speed. Another hundred feet down this tight gorge a further boulder split the torrent into two curls of aerated water that were ejected into the final raceway of the runnel. We stood on platforms above this savage stretch of water in awe.

I turned to Skip. 'Grade six?'

'Grade six and up!' he roared exuberantly, making gestures symbolic of death and the life ever after.

We jumped over a foaming side stream and traversed a hundred yards of alluvial stockpiling to another spectacular twist in the river's humour. An island outcrop had caused the river to bifurcate, encircling it with wild rapids that swept past in a series of smooth pulsing stopper waves before reuniting and rushing towards the lip of the waterfall and the spray of the anvil stone below.

The glacier met the river above here and to go on we had to scurry across its moraine-clad surfaces as we moved up the bank. The river made a long bend to the north beyond a quicksand beach and it appeared that this was where it entered the main gorge and where the Chong Kumdan Glacier had created the great glacial dam that in the past had periodically broken, sending walls of water flooding down with catastrophic consequences in the lower Shyok and Indus Valleys. It was getting late, so we decided to turn back, when Terry spied an empty jerry-can that must have been swept down from the military camp at Gapshan beyond the gorge. Reconnaissance and maturity evaporated as we were all struck by a spontaneous outbreak of schoolboy stone-throwing. Seldom has a jerry-can been so abused and battered.

Retracing our steps we crossed the Kichik Kumdan Glacier and the sand flats above the red cathedral wall, our weary feet beginning to drag as we moved through the vastness of this gigantic environment. By the time we reached the Au Tash Glacier its meltwater stream was in full milky flood, cascading over the rocks we had used as stepping-stones in the morning. The once pleasant little brook was now a raging torrent. One by one we carefully positioned ourselves on the bank, studied the rocks that were still above water-level for their suitability as stepping-stones-cum-landing-pads and, after a spell of deep breathing, launched ourselves into an Olympic-standard hop-skip-and-jump. My first hop fell short, but there was no stopping in mid-manoeuvre and several splashdowns later I had entertained my more sure-footed companions and could wring out my socks.

When we got back to camp Prem told us a message had come through from the military saying that our pony caravan

from Sasoma had not reached Skyangpoche. Further enquir-
ies were thwarted because the telephone line down-valley
was reported 'u.s.': unserviceable. The only hope lay in
the bright suggestion that the severed connection was a
consequence of one of our ponies treading on the telephone
cable, which would at least mean they were on the way.

I woke on our third morning at Saser Brangsa to the rapid
high-pitched call of the ram chikor, the mountain pheasant;
a small finch was chirping from its boulder-top perch to the
south; the Shyok River roared far below, while near at hand
came the drip of melting snow as it trickled off the roof of
the tent and the sound of the nylon springing taut in the
sun. The beginning of a new day.

It was a rest day, to be spent reading, writing, washing
clothes and in some cases body and soul, too. Though the
isolation is an accepted factor in such an expedition as ours,
missing one's loved ones is still a hard part of a long journey.

Already that recurrent expedition conversational theme of
food and drink had cropped up. Occasionally the talk would
digress to other topics but it always seemed to return to those
culinary delights and luxuries that one missed most. Miriam
told us the thing she wanted was a great big bathtub filled
with hot water, to which Skip commented that he, personally,
would prefer a bathtub filled to the brim with champagne. I
readily agreed with this fantasy although there were some
more coarse among us who declared their preference for
beer. Miriam, undeterred, continued to tell us that she and
Renée intended to go to a beauty parlour when they returned
to civilisation after the expedition.

'Why? Do they sell beer there?' Brett asked.

In the early afternoon a portly officer, followed by two
tough-looking Ladakhis, came strolling along the track. He
was a major stationed at Chong Tash and going on leave
after one year's continuous service in this remote area. He
was not surprisingly looking forward to returning to his

home on the plains. After all, he added, the winter temperature range at Chong Tash was -10 to -50°C.

During the previous few days we had seen large transport
aircraft circling over the Chong Tash area and we asked the
major what was happening.

'Oh, they are doing the air drop. They do it every day that
the weather is fine,' he said, twisting the waxed tips of his
long stringy moustache. 'You know, they have to do it again
and again because half of the parachutes do not open.' He
wobbled his head in that characteristic way, wished us the
best of luck and marched off along the track swinging his
walking-stick.

Prem and Tara returned from the army post where they
had managed to talk with Wangchuk over the telephone. He
was above Skyangpoche and planned to reach Saser Brangsa
with the pony caravan the next day, so Prem thought we
should move our camp down to the banks of the river near
the flying-fox cable-way, all ready to begin ferrying the loads
across as soon as Wangchuk's caravan joined us. This decision did much to raise the morale of the group gathered
round the yak-dung fire that night, and next morning we
broke camp and after a twenty-minute trek, piled all our gear
near the decrepit rope-way and its even more precarious
basket. This seemed to be an outstanding opportunity for us
to lose a great deal of our equipment to the rushing waters
of the Shyok.

PV drew me aside. He looked most concerned and it was
clear that he had to get something of immense importance
off his chest. Again it was the security of the Indian sub-
continent that was at stake, and the centre of vulnerability
was the flying-fox rope-way. We were stunned. Could this
heap of moribund machinery be top security? He assured me
that it was and proceeded to explain how crucial it was to
the defence of the entire area. The bottom line was that
photography was restricted. With this momentous statement
PV began to turn puce, which he usually did when he got

on to the subject of security arrangements and our inability to take them as seriously as they deserved. This was a disappointment but after so many disappointments already we had developed an enormous capacity to cope with, and be excruciatingly philosophical about, such setbacks. There was nothing else for it. We would play a gentleman's game of cricket, immediately, to show what good sports we all were.

It was a grand slam match between two competitive teams, the Rimo Rankers and the Shyok Shirkers. The boundaries were set using a dried-up stream-bed to the east, the Shyok River to the south, a tall moraine wall to the north and a steep bank to the west. Any balls hit beyond these boundaries were worth four runs unless the umpire awarded six for a ball that appeared to have exceptional inertia as it flew by. JP, Errol and Terry were the bowlers to be watched and the leading batsmen as well, plus Prem, who would belt the ball with such force that he accumulated a succession of fours, each time giggling uproariously. The game was in full swing and the teams were battling for the lead, when Magan shouted, 'The ponies are coming.'

It was Wangchuk and two of the pony wallahs at last. The remainder of the caravan would arrive in the morning. But the bad news was that most of the fuel, some of our tin trunks and all the rafting equipment had been left in Sasoma, and would follow, we were assured, in dribs and drabs. The rafts were being left for Jack Morrison to bring on with him when he arrived in a couple of weeks. So the expedition was, arguably, more dispersed than ever and though we would have most of the critical food and equipment by the following day, the missing 'tin trunk caravan' began to develop some notoriety.

We spent the evening going through the expedition accounts, an exercise that proved rather convoluted as a variety of assurances had apparently been given by different expedition members on behalf of the Rimo Expedition both to people who were actively working for us and to some who were not (one had gone on holiday in Tibet), and all wanted to be paid as per the agreement. No one could remember who had given which assurance, nor when they gave it. What was clear was that there were some locals among those who organised the ponies who wanted to make a lot of money. The man who had gone off to Tibet wanted a ten per cent cut of the entire expedition budget, plus a fee and food, and he planned to charge each of the pony wallahs twenty per cent of what they made because he had given them the job. This meant that Tenzing Dorje and his aides planned to charge the expedition about twenty-five per cent of the entire budget for their services. Bankruptcy loomed until we unanimously agreed to alter the wages scheme due to lack of any evidence of an agreement and with that we retired to bed wondering what it had all been about in the first place. Tenzing Dorje's absence did not mean he was going to let our decision be carried easily, as we found later. Tenzing had been commissioned by Terry to organise the ponies which he had done by degrees as a side-line to his primary school teaching career and, of course, to holidaying in Tibet. He was from Deshkit, near where the Nubra joined the Shyok Valley but had little experience of working with horses and large numbers of people.

We spent the next day hauling our loads over the cable-way. It was hard work, slow and tedious and, amazingly, we had a few close calls but no disasters and nothing went missing. A long rope was tied to the platform-cum-basket that was suspended beneath the wire cable by two greased pulley-wheels. With enormous quantities of effort the gear was drawn across the river to a cacophony of chants and yells. To our absolute astonishment the rest of the ponies started arriving around mid-day and with them came the 'tin trunk caravan' and the floors of the rafts. The rafts themselves remained in Sasoma. But the pony wallahs were not at all open to dialogue regarding the speedy recommencement of our journey along the Silk Road. This struck us all as the final blow in a series of setbacks and tempers were becoming increasingly frayed. Prem laid down the law to these recalcitrants, assuring them that unless they co-operated he would make life very difficult for them through his army contacts in the area. Fortunately they recognised the wisdom of co-operation at this point and agreed to put in long days from the next day on. With that they continued to lead their ponies up on to the mountainsides to areas of scattered pasture. Brett and I found ourselves arguing with PV which brought an unsatisfactory day to an unsatisfactory conclusion.

PV carried out the job of liaison officer as a security agent infiltrating our ranks for the army and for his country, instead of as a liaison between ourselves and the country we were moving through which is what the job is supposed to be about. He was patriotic to the point of fanaticism and suspicious to the extent of paranoia. He had already suggested that Magan, one of India's stronger mountaineers, was a Pakistani spy and that we might all have subversive aspirations in this northern region, suggesting connections with the CIA and the Australian and New Zealand national security agencies. When pressed to substantiate these accusations he conceded that the security breach might occur when we returned home. He described the likely scenario where men in black suits from some intelligence service would knock on my door and pleasantly show interest in our expedition and ask if they could see our photographs. Whereupon they would almost certainly locate shots of immense importance to Indian security. I found these suggestions as irritating as they were hysterical and told him so. Why had we been given permission by the Government of India, including the Department of Defence, if we constituted such a security hazard? It was one of those arguments that was never going to be satisfactorily resolved.

Prem gathered our frustrated little band together for some

hot rum and hors d'oeuvres as we sat cross-legged on the gravel outside his tent. A flush of bonhomie developed as our meagre rum supply was steadily depleted. The temperature began to drop so we erected the Kelty dome tent and drowned our frustrations in more booze and a disco. Renée, wearing hot pink leotards and a pair of spectacles with large white plastic eyeballs gyrating on the end of two springs, flung herself around the tent more or less to the rhythm of the punk music that our recently arrived speakers pumped out but to which everyone was oblivious. Then Miriam came in, her eyelids shimmering with blue eye make-up and a horse's thigh-bone tied across her neck as a bow-tie. There was multidecibel applause. Most of us were now wearing some of our mountain clothing which tends to be brightly coloured, so we looked a tent full of court jesters. The pitch of intoxi-cation escalated until Wangchuk attempted to emulate Renée's dance, remaining upright with great difficulty, and Tara insisted on pounding on the aluminium cooking pots, creating a deafening din. The prospect of moving on next day after six nights stuck at Saser Brangsa was clearly rendering us manic with relief.

5

The Gates of Hell
25 – 27 August

The only members of the expedition who were less than enthusiastic about moving on next morning were our ponies, who were not keen on swimming across the fast-flowing and very cold Shyok river. Rocks and abuse, hurled in liberal quantities, forced them to negotiate the rapids and scramble ashore on the far side. In swimming the 150-foot-wide river they drifted downstream about two hundred yards, and it was a pathetic mob of horses that stood shivering while the pony wallahs loaded our equipment before continuing on along the river flat on our way to Murgo.

Jonga had overlooked producing breakfast for all of us and had not prepared any lunch provisions for the day's trek. Much to the irritation of the pony men, we rummaged through the loads of the moving horses looking for items considered edible and accessible.

Clumps of hardy flowers and alpine rhubarb grew along the track which we followed to where it jack-knifed its way up an exposed outcrop at the entrance to a gorge. The route led us north-east and away from the prison of the Shyok Valley, traversing vast scree slides until we could look south-east into a broad valley cradled by exotic peaks, and see a suggestion of some pasture. This was the valley of Chong Tash. Skip and I sat on a protruding spur and gazed across at this strangely hospitable vale. Dave, Renée and PV joined us and together we descended the flank into the narrow gut. Here a swift stream swept over the pebble bed that made up the floor of the canyon and we followed it downstream a short way, leaping across where the water met the cliff-face. Around one bend we met the pony caravan which had come up the stream-bed from the Shyok. We followed them up a wash-out on the southern side of the gorge and out on to the Chong Tash Valley which we wandered across, enjoying the gentle angle of the meadow and the pastel pinks of the crags above. Near a shallow brown lake with a smear of crystalline salt on its shores we halted for lunch which we shared with Prem and Magan. During this pleasant break a huge Russian-made helicopter, an MI8, flew slowly overhead, beating the thin air with resonant sweeps of its great blades, and disappeared down-valley towards the Chong Tash military camp. That sense of being comfortably alone evaporated, we packed up, and continued on our way.

We marched beyond our valley horizon and inexorably into a war zone that shocked all but Prem. A mile away we could see Chong Tash army camp; the mud bunkers draped with white parachute cloths from thousands of successful and disastrous air drops. The evidence for the failures lay all around us and off to one side a timeless horse and cart picked through the twentieth-century rubbish deluged upon that alpine meadow by modern aviation. There must have been tens of thousands of concertina-ed jerry-cans and boxes of tinned food whose parachutes had failed to open, sending them screaming to the ground and, often as not, obliterating another of the diminishing number of alpine shrubs and herbs. Beside the brook that drained the valley the military had made a half-hearted attempt at concentrating the debris of destroyed jerry-cans. The pile was ten feet high and snaked along the banks of the stream for about a mile. The meadow was an appalling rubbish dump. Looking up we found that even the mountainsides were graffiti-ed. Whitewashed letters two hundred feet tall proclaimed SHOOT TO KILL,

JULLAY and O MANE PADME HUM. Presumably these messages made the soldiers feel invincible and, no doubt, amused foreign satellite operators.

While Prem went into the camp (and did not receive a particularly warm welcome from his fellow officers) we were escorted past it by a sullen-faced sergeant whose generally unpleasant attitude made it pretty clear that Brett was being unduly optimistic when he had hoped that they would offer us some tea. I, for one, was not sorry to leave the desecration that was Chong Tash.

At the junction of two valleys we reached Murgo, the Indo-Tibetan Border Police camp in the area, nestled beneath a cluster of tall red pinnacles. In contrast to Chong Tash the men at Murgo were most hospitable, giving us tea and a warm tent to sit in while we rested. Terry and I drafted a message for Prem to send to Jogindar Singh in New Delhi via the ITBP radio to ensure that Jack Morrison did not have to repeat the delays we had experienced during the past several weeks and to notify Delhi of our progress. From Murgo we marched into the Gates of Hell.

Craggy peaks crowded in on the track as it traversed steep tallus slides and crossed deep nalas. On a sculptured prominence encrusted with siliceous deposits, bubbled the transparency of mineral springs. The water had smeared the smooth contours of the mound with beautiful elemental colours and cascaded in a veil to a river that lay in the seclusion of a precipitous canyon which cut a sinuous course below. I stopped briefly to fill my water bottle from the mineral pools, that were filled with the strange waving shapes of green algae, before wandering on feeling more and more enchanted by my surroundings. The track cut across another flank and dropped down into the gorge itself where I was joined by Dave and Renée. We traced the meandering canyon floor to a bluff where we were forced to climb fifty feet of unstable rock to regain a tenuous track that had appeared above us. I watched Dave help Renée, who is no climber, scale this bluff and he did it with great patience and care. Once reunited with the trail we scrambled on, crossing more scree slopes and ledges above the river. Periodically we stopped and gazed ahead at the mountain wall that barred the end of the valley. This geological oddity was like an operatic stage-drop, the mythical representation of a mountain by a designer who has never seen one. The theatrical mountain wall was the creation of fantasy and an appropriate setting for *Faust* or *Lord of the Rings*. It exuded the unreality of a giant slice of pink whale's blubber streaked with blood. Following the crest of the mountain was a tier of ice-cliffs that gleamed in the rich evening light. Turning our gaze back to the track we slowly trudged on the last few hundred yards to a platform above the river where we were to camp. Already most of the ponies were being unloaded and some had already been led to a perilously steep scree slide across the river where there was, apparently, some scant feed for these hardy creatures. The mountainside was so steep that should a pony lose its footing it would roll unimpeded into the canyon below. I hoped the pony wallahs knew what they were doing.

Dinner-time brought a surprise. Our mascot, Grindlay the goat, had found the day's trek too much for him and had had to be carried the last few hours to camp where he was consigned to the cooking pot. So it was with mixed feelings that we ate our goat curry and ubiquitous dhal bhat that night as we huddled under the cook tarpaulin with large snowflakes falling thickly outside. We had all begun to disperse to our tents when out of the darkness appeared PV who had, once again, gone missing. He had visited the army camp and obtained some more dhal bhat for the expedition which a soldier had carried for him to this spot. But he was in an exceptionally bad temper as he was wet and cold and feeling neglected.

'Why did a search party not come to my rescue?' he demanded.

I tried, as did Errol, to reason with him but he had already gone that dreaded puce colour and was unapproachable. I wished him *bon appétit* as a bowl of hot Grindlay was handed to him, and retired to my tent.

I lay in my sleeping bag listening to the pitter-patter of the snow on the roof and my mind drifted to what lay ahead and what lay behind. I wondered how Ann was faring back in Australia and I missed some of the old routines of giving the horses their buckets of oats and chaff and feeding out hay from the tractor to the cattle. I summoned up Woodend, the little farm cottage where we lived, and the gaudy-coloured rosellas and parakeets that fly around the back door scavenging on spilt horsefeed, the dogs and all those pleasantly familiar things that make up one's day-to-day life at home. How much a part of my life they had become and how these thoughts exacerbated my sense of isolation. I doubt there is anywhere more remote than the Gates of Hell.

Next morning most of the caravan left promptly and I was happy to hear that all the ponies were accounted for. I walked along behind enjoying the peace of solitude and recalling the legend Prem had told us about the Gates of Hell. The wild red mountain was once the grand castle of a young warrior. He had hidden a princess there with whom he had absconded and prepared for the princess's father, the local king, to attack him. He had burned all the forests and grassland that surrounded the castle so that the king's horses would have nothing to graze on and this fire had caused the rocks to bleed and turn red.

The poppy red of the wall's fresh cleavages and eroded prows and pinnacles was not of this world. And as I followed the track I passed over ravines only a few feet wide and a hundred feet deep. The limited rainfall in this area makes such confined slots sufficient to drain the mountain flanks and the slender canyons that branch from this valley.

Ahead I could see a string of our ponies moving steadily

up the gorge, traversing sweeping flanks and disappearing from view as they filed into another ravine. Again and again I crossed the deep ravines that sliced into the flanks of the red mountain, leading up its side like abysmal hallways through which only starving men could pass. Further on the valley narrowed and was choked by landslides. The river flowed through these barriers and the pony caravan clambered unquestioningly around, over and through the giant boulder chaos. Through one of these diabolical constrictions we filed and found ourselves ejected on to a vast river flat that seemed to go on for ever. We set out across this enjoying the ability to walk alongside one another and talk as we went.

Roddy told me that PV had warned them to avoid any metal objects we found on the track, as the previous day a soldier had been killed by picking up an old Chinese hand-grenade. His funeral was today at the army camp at Burtsa, just a few hours up the track. Again the reality of being in a war zone was driven home as we trekked on across the great river flats, void of any vegetation or people but occasionally scattered with the debris of the military – jerry-cans, an old piston, fragments of machinery.

An hour later the smooth going came to an abrupt halt where a gigantic landslide had swept across the valley. Looking up we could see fresh breaks a few thousand feet above. As the resulting debris had travelled several miles across the valley, the momentum must have been enormous. Through this obstacle the river had cut a labyrinthine course which, at times, became a maze of caverns where we found pools filled with polished stones of every hue: lime green, lavender, lilac, pale pink and blood red. Terry had always been interested in gemstones and the idea of finding something that makes you rich overnight was particularly appealing. From his pack he pulled a geological hammer and proceeded to work his way along the river-bed in search of the mother lode. But we reached the far side of the landslide debris as impecunious as we were when we started our prospecting.

A gorge to be negotiated near Chong Tash.

The Gates of Hell, above, the wall near Murgo and, below, the ponies negotiating the gorge beyond.

The breath-taking expanse of the Depsang Plains above, and below, figures dwarfed in their endless folds.

High-altitude cricket. Brett's bowling action improved at 17,000 feet.

Moss growing at 18,000 feet on the Depsang Plains.

A farrier shoes a reluctant pony.

A fit of rare and chilling cleanliness for Skip in a stream near the Chip Chap River.

Our caravan trails down toward the Chip Chap.

Rimo at last, looking up the South Rimo Glacier from Base Camp.

A spectacular avalanche above the South Rimo Glacier.

Our first serious look at the South-East Ridge.

Prem at Advance Base with Rimo beyond.

Dave, Brett, Terry and Skip at Camp 1 at the foot of the South Face.

Rajiv and Roddy at Advance Base during the reconnaissance.

Peter seeks encouragement before load-carrying on our return journey.

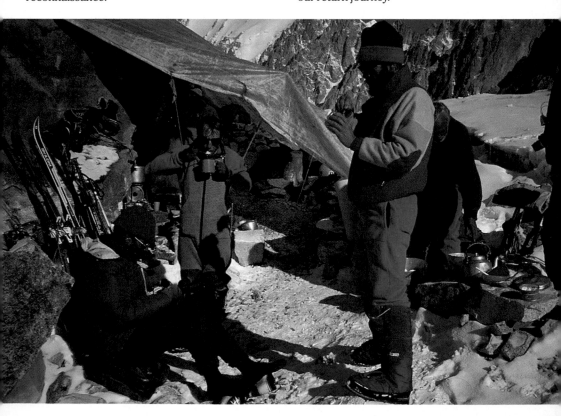

Prem, Brett and Skip breakfasting at Advance Base.

This spot had been an unhappy one for a small group of Indian soldiers during the 1962 war with China as there had been a battle here in which they had suffered heavy casualties. Poignantly, there was now tranquillity and a few blades of green grass where once there had been conflict.

Out in the middle of the expansive river flat that led us in a gentle bend to the north we stopped to have some lunch. In the distance we could make out the small army encampment of Burtsa, a cluster of parachute-cloth-covered huts on the south side of a shallow ridge that extended out on to the great river plain. As we looked we saw a dozen tiny figures moving on the gravel flats in the foreground and they appeared to be coming our way. Non-plussed we went on munching on our chapattis and Roddy, the self-appointed caretaker of the Vegemite jar, allotted minuscule scoops of this precious spread to be dispensed among us.

The soldiers jogged towards us and even from a distance we could see that they were heavily armed. Happily, they were a friendly lot who all shook us by the hands and after a few niceties continued on their way down-valley. One of them told us that they were going on leave in Leh. We watched them jog into the distance. There was little doubt they were very fit for they were running at 15,000 feet and most of them were wearing large pneumatic gumboots. They carried sten guns, mortar guns and an Indian version of the AK47 and they all had that serious air of men who knew how to use them.

For three hours we marched along the river plain that meandered through the rubble mountains towards the Depsang Plains. North of Burtsa we passed some strange alluvial tors that stood out on the river flat as testimony to another landslide that had been cleared by the river and time itself. Just when I was wondering where we were going to stop, we rounded a bend and before me was a strip of green grass beneath a large moraine and already erected on the sward were a few of our tents. We were at 16,000 feet and the area was desolate and inhospitable, particularly for our horses who would find little to fill their bellies here.

It was four in the afternoon and we were soon swilling cups of sweet stewed tea and munching glucose biscuits. An officer travelling down-valley stopped and told us of the rigours of the Depsang Plains as his surly foot soldier stood by with his sten gun slung over his shoulder. After erecting our own tents Skip, Terry, Roddy and I walked out on to the river plain to search for some of the legendary Burtsa stones, a spherical or elliptical stone that looks as if it could be the internal moulding of a sea egg. We strutted around the great plain with our eyes to the ground, frequently muttering another of our team jokes, 'This is a good place for the Burtsa stone.' We were not finding any and so our assertions were all the more ludicrous. Once when I was in Delhi visiting a friend, I had admired the many trees I had seen in the streets of the city. 'Yes, Delhi is a good place for the trees,' he had replied. It seemed such a profound observation of something so very evident that I had remembered it and it had now become part of the jargon of the Rimo Expedition. The term had engendered a whole selection of affirmations and contradictions about things we had seen along the way.

'Here's one!' I roared. 'This is a good place for the Burtsa stone.' The others rushed over to where I had found the cricket-ball-sized speckled stone, muttering a number of versions of the current mantra. 'If you are looking for the Burtsa stone, this is a good place.'

We all returned to our tents early that night in preparation for the long day we expected while crossing the Depsang Plains. My tent was pitched alongside the pony wallahs' tent, and tethered all around it were the ponies so that our departure would not be delayed by the need to muster the animals from the mountainsides in the morning. So not for the last time my sleep was disturbed by the tinkling of their bells as they moved round all night to keep warm. Feeling rather decrepit I rose at five-thirty to pack away my frost-covered tent and to have breakfast. With almost alarming efficiency the pony wallahs had the ponies laden with their fifty-kilo loads and we were on our way, the camp completely evacuated of its sixty ponies and twenty-five humans by 7.00 a.m.

Brett and Terry were not feeling well, so Dave and I were taking on the principal roles in making the expedition film. The large 8-mm camera had developed an appetite for chewing up our precious film and an uncanny knack of doing this at the worst times. Ponies are difficult creatures to choreograph and so it's either *cinéma verité* or nothing. Dave and I marched up the river flat discussing our camera ideas and the current problems and as we went the topography changed. The broad flats narrowed, requiring repeated crossing of the river. We were gaining altitude steadily too as honeycombed bluffs advanced in on the river-banks. Perhaps some of these caverns would have been used as shelters by the old traders and, perhaps, the ibex hunters whose rock etchings had impressed us earlier in the trek. I noted that much of the rock was a poor quality conglomerate and breccia, the detritus of glaciation and other erosive forces that have carved this extraordinary landscape over millions of years. Further on were polished boulders of hardened conglomerate, almost psychedelic in the colours of their constituent pebbles, rocks and sands. I could hardly believe my eyes as we stood among these fairytale stones. One almost expected something magical to happen.

Here the gorge narrowed to a canyon only twenty feet wide and the route ascended away from the crag-enclosed river-bed that was now little more than a small stream. We followed the confines of this bottle-neck gulch, stepping from boulder to fantastic boulder as we ascended its circuitous twists to where it abruptly gave out on to the gentle rolls of a changed topography. We had left the vertical gullies of the main valleys behind us and ahead rose the smooth white features of the high plains of Central Asia.

6

Across the Depsang Plains
27 – 30 August

A shallow hollow led for nearly 2000 feet to where the glistening white rubble landscape met the sky and the lip of the Depsang Plains. We plodded for an hour up this long synclinal fold in the Depsang's flank, breathing deeply in the air of nearly 18,000 feet. An insignificant niche in the skyline, marked by a pile of stones from which protruded a tuft of weather-beaten prayer flags, indicated the pass on to which we clambered. The wind whistled from the north-west chilling our hands and ears and I could feel tears well in my eyes as much from the cold as from the emotion of reaching this forbidden plain. The rolling platform of the plains stretched for mile upon mile to the north.

Beyond rose a range of snowless peaks, all about 22,000 feet (6500 metres) high and lying in Tibet. Just two miles from where we stood was the Chinese border and Prem assured us that they would be watching our every move. I could see nothing worth fighting over here. It was harsh, magnificent country but worthless for anything other than boosting the military ego. We lingered as long as we were allowed, gazing out across the plain and into the brown bronze of the mountain plateaux in China. Again there was the skeletal evidence of the rigours involved in these high plain crossings. A huge camel skull and assorted bleached bones lay among the rocks but although we were at 18,000 feet there was no snow.

Dropping off the pass we traversed below the crest and into an indent in the flank from where a spring slowly seeped. A thick felt of green grass grew around the water source and beyond this only the tortoiseshell shape of hardy mounds of moss prospered. We were out of the wind here so our large group sprawled upon that green carpet and spent a pleasant luncheon siesta. The sun was strong and warm and it soon returned the circulation to my chilled extremities as I lay gazing out over the splintered peaks that fringed the valleys up which we had come from the south. Feeling refreshed we sauntered on over the rolling terrain that was curiously striped with vertical parallel lines, about a foot apart and caused, presumably, by thousands of years of snowmelt action. Everywhere in this strange land there were features that were different from what any of us had seen before and so our progress became more akin to loitering than purposeful trekking.

The Depsang's perimeter was a collar of undulating desert ridges from which we could look out over an ever-growing panorama and our ecstatic use of our cameras reflected its impact on us. Roddy produced his Widelux, 140-degree, wide-angle camera and we soon lost account of time. Great tracts of desolate mountain scenery spread around us and to the west rose a wall of snow-capped peaks with glaciers that tumbled down to the plain to extend white tongues upon the floor of desolation. We were surrounded by the mountainous borders of India, Pakistan and China and not too far distant were the borders of Russia and Afghanistan. We felt as if we were balanced on a fulcrum of no-man's-land. Some of the soldiers had told us that in winter the temperatures dropped to -50°C in this area and that there were strong winds; not surprisingly the posting was not popular. Yet despite the severity of the environment, we found hoofprints and drop-pings of ibex and burrel.

It was getting late and still no sign of the ponies or camp. Both PV and Renée were running low on energy, so Skip,

Dave and I took some of Renée's load and asked PV to let us do the same for him.

'Oh, no. I will keep coming slowly,' he said, looking unsteady on his feet.

'Stop and drink something, PV.'

But he assured me he was not thirsty.

'PV, you can't not be thirsty. You haven't drunk anything since lunch-time. Drink some of this.' I offered my water bottle, realising as I did so that he may have some caste prohibitions on sharing such things. He refused so we encouraged him over to a brook and gave him some boiled sweets to suck.

The gully led up nearly a thousand feet to a pass at over 18,000 feet where we stepped out on to the level expanse of the Depsang Plains. Skip and I were delighted to be there but at the same time keen to be off the plain, too, as a piercingly cold wind blasted across it and the sun was already low on the horizon, casting long elegant shadows off the peaks. The quite anachronistic tableland swept before us, an undulating rubble platform of expansive proportions, and had it not been for a line of cairns that stood in lonely vigil upon the plain we would not have been sure which way to go.

Periodically we found prints of horses' hooves in the gravel and sometimes droppings, which were welcome signs. We had decided that the two of us would proceed ahead of the others to find the route, so that when darkness came we would be able to guide the rest of the group. After several miles of trudging in the steady blast of the north-west wind the cairned route dropped away off the western lip of the Depsang. Descending below the table-top of the plain we shed the vulnerability we had felt out on that exposed plateau and as we lost altitude, entered a deep gully, draining west, that ultimately joined a valley system that drained north into the Chip Chap River. From this point we began to be able to see something of our destination, the snout of the South

Rimo Glacier embedded in grey moraine and to the right the heavily sérac-ed terminus of the Central Rimo Glacier. Draining these two great bodies of ice was the Shyok River which appeared a braided combination of swollen streams. Beyond in a maelstrom of wind and cloud was Rimo, and although we could not see the summit we could clearly see the lower sections of the distinctive spurs that frame the East Face of the mountain. To the south lay a small notch in the ridge and before long the sun shone its final rays through the sights of this col, highlighting the swirling cloud about the Rimo Massif.

Rajiv and Brett joined us and we scanned the broad valley below that already lay in the gloom of evening.

'There they are!' Rajiv pointed into the growing darkness below and near a stream we could see some light-coloured objects that were probably our tents. It had been a long hard day, twelve hours altogether, and two very high passes were behind us. Later, as I drained the tomato soup from my mug, Brett called, 'Look over there!'

An intense white flash soared down across the dark north-eastern sky and disappeared behind the horizon of the Depsang Plains. Behind it lingered an incandescent trail of milk-coloured cloud. Had ET landed on the Depsang? It seemed more likely to be military activity or a satellite racing through a cloud of upper atmosphere dust.

'The Chinese have tested missiles and bombs over there somewhere,' Terry observed.

'It could be the start of another Indo-Chinese war,' some-one suggested.

'That would be the end of an expedition that has only just begun,' put in Dave's Yorkshire accent.

'No. That is not possible,' was the response of the typically emphatic Magan.

The next day, 28 August, was decreed to be a necessary rest day for humans and animals alike. After Wangchuk brought round the pre-breakfast cup of coffee I unzipped my tent and watched one of the pony wallahs emerge from their tent nearby with a blackened pot in his hand. He was wearing the traditional maroon cloak, a sturdy woollen garment that reached down to his knees, and on his head an ancient woollen cap. Scattered all around their tent was the horse gear: the hand-made wooden harnesses and woollen horse rugs dyed red and decorated with blue-and-yellow motifs. This equine equipment hasn't changed for centuries and, apart from some of our plastic barrels and waxed cardboard boxes bearing the expedition insignia, the scene I looked out upon must have been identical to those that Marco Polo experienced when he passed through the Pamirs just north of here in the thirteenth century. Beyond the pony wallah, who was now scouring the pot with gravel from the stream, stood the barren mountains north of the Chip Chap River that constituted another border with China. North of this range lay the Sinkiang and the isolated towns of Yarkand and Kashgar.

Once the quarter-inch of snow had melted people sloped off to the stream with towels and soap and that look of intent that precedes an action requiring great determination. The net effect was considerable as shampooed hair and washed faces changed several people's appearances completely, particularly Roddy who was seen jumping about in a theatrical way, stark naked, in the snow meltwater and Errol and Skip who made alarming noises when they washed their hair. It was debated that some of these people never recovered from this experience and others maintained it did them a world of good.

In the meantime the pony wallahs got on with the serious business of repairing some of their gear and shoeing the horses after the rough terrain had taken its toll. Few of the horses would stand for the farrier and so they had to be man-handled to the ground by five pony wallahs where their legs were bound with a leather strap. The five men then sat on the incapacitated creature while the farrier got on with his work. The shoes were simple affairs, but effective, and the tools of trade were not too different to what is used in the stables of Europe and Australasia. The farrier filed and clipped the hoof to improve its shape and then pounded five nails in to secure the new shoe.

In the early afternoon we climbed on to a platform above the stream to thrash out another match of high-altitude cricket. The rival elevens were the Depsang Devils and the Chip Chap Chaps. The lunacy of playing cricket at 17,000 feet (5000 metres) was emphasised by the white cricket hats that Terry insisted we all wear.

'It just wouldn't be cricket, mate.'

We marked out a twenty-two-yard pitch and pounded the wickets into the concrete-hard ground at each end, balancing the bails carefully on top. At all of this Skip looked on with New World bemusement. 'And what do you call this? I guess the rules are based on baseball?'

Such comments are of course an open invitation to any cricket fanatic to start explaining the rules, which Errol and Terry did with missionary fervour to the increasingly perplexed Skip, and any pony wallahs misguided enough to stray too close and get recruited for the match.

We used a real red leather cricket ball and whether it was the thin air of these high plains or merely the vigour of the bowlers, I do not know, but the speed of the bowling was terrifying. But not to JP, Errol, Terry and Prem who sent that red ball flying high above the outstretched hands of the fieldsmen/women and off down the slope to the stream. Stopdan, one of our leading pony wallahs, had a baseball chuck that was applauded only by Skip. It simply wasn't cricket, but had to be allowed for diplomatic reasons which was, ultimately, a mistake, for Stopdan proceeded to demolish the Depsang Devils using his accuracy at throwing stones at horses. Eventually this *was* decreed 'Not cricket', and he was disqualified.

Terry and I played a demonstration over for the film camera, in which Terry was bowled out while he was complying with Dave's wish for him to produce a cloud of dust with his bat. This dismissal was hotly contested, but the umpire, Prem, ruled him out and the Depsang Devils lost their last decent batsman, having already lost Errol. JP proceeded to belt the ball for four with monotonous regularity, taking the Chip Chap Chaps to a decisive win which he conceded with a nod of his turbaned head. 'A close match, Peter.'

The match was almost certainly the highest game of cricket ever played. And, by implication, we must have been the only people silly enough to take cricket gear to such a place.

I had to have one last look at the Depsang Plains before we left the next day. No one else seemed particularly enthused, so I set off alone up the long gradual slope behind our cricket pitch. Moving quickly I gained the lip of the plain in forty-five minutes and walked off across its remarkable horizontal surface. So strange a place was it that I felt I could be somewhere as remote and curious as on the moon.

A strong cold wind blew, as it had done before, encouraging me to walk more quickly over the pebble-studded surface. Examining the pebbles more closely, some were etched, others had unusual nodules on them, some were coated with a dark brown glaze and others still were cleaved and split. Presumably the elements were responsible for these unusual shapes and effects, they certainly had the appearance of rocks that had been subjected to great extremes. I returned to the edge of the plain and with a final look at this astonishing place began my descent to our camp far below. A shallow nala led me directly down the massive flanks and as I went I watched carefully for any signs of wildlife. Tiny hoofprints trailed across the slope and in the gully were the burrows and droppings of rabbits. A few little brown birds flew off before me but otherwise nothing. I told Skip about the birds when I returned. But he couldn't put a name to them either, so for the rest of the trip they became confidently referred to as LBBs – little brown birds.

It was a clear night and the temperature dropped to -15°C which kept the ponies tethered around the pony wallahs' tent, tramping about all night with their woollen rugs and pack harnesses in place as an added protection against the intense cold, and I was kept awake once more by the jingling of the bells on their embroidered collars, as they tossed their heads and buried their noses in their hessian nosebags.

Next morning we descended to the Chip Chap River. It was a little larger than the stream we had been camped beside over the past two days, but it had cut a broken cleft fifty to a hundred feet deep in the base of a very broad, concave watershed. To the north lay the rocky range that constituted the border with China and to the left we could glimpse the vast river flats of the Upper Shyok. We were photographing away enthusiastically when PV came up to us with that urgent look written on his face that is commonly associated with matters of great importance or gastro-enteritis.

'Dave, Peter. No more filming is allowed!'

'Why?' We echoed one another with that infuriatingly Western response.

'Two soldiers have come from the Gapshan army camp with the orders from the commanding officer. They are saying no more photographs are allowed in this area. We are being escorted from here to avoid the security risk.'

We weren't happy but what could we do? We knew there was nothing that PV could do either.

'They will be watching us. I can assure you. This is the army. They will be very strict,' he went on, wobbling his head from side to side in that most Indian movement. 'They are saying that Colonel and me also are not permitted to go to Gapshan.'

'That's ridiculous, PV, you're both Indian Army Officers. It's an insult to you as our liaison officer and from the Northern Command, too.'

'I think this must be so.' PV stood there on that desolate flank, still wobbling his head. 'The soldier told me he had the orders not to tell me anything.'

'Your orders in Leh were to send radio messages from Gapshan. What will you do about that?'

'I will speak to Colonel. He is my senior officer.'

I left the unhappy PV and strode off down the slope to the river feeling both perplexed and frustrated by his news. Jumping from boulder to boulder with limited success I reached the far side annoyed and wet. Two soldiers eyed me carefully, no doubt expecting me to pull out my camera at any moment and start snapping. They were lean, fit-looking fellows, almost certainly uneducated villagers from the foot-hills. An order was an order to these men, there would be no qualification or interpretation. I decided that simple-minded silence was the best solution.

When Terry descended to join me he told me that one of our ponies had collapsed and miscarried before his eyes. The pony wallahs decided to leave the mare in the Chip Chap Valley to recover and to collect her on their way back to Sasoma in a few days.

'We're working these little ponies pretty hard,' Terry said. 'Some of them are carrying sixty kilos which at these altitudes is hard going.'

He was right; they were all looking weary and many had nasty sores on their rumps and shoulders caused by the loads. They were like Welsh mountain ponies without the condition. I would guess their weight to be about two hun-dred kilos and going down day by day.

The soldiers led us down the Chip Chap a short distance and off across a spur that formed the northern bank of the river. Much of the ground had salt lying on the surface and consequently there was little vegetation.

'Even if we run out of everything else, we can still have salt,' boomed Prem. 'We can send Jonga down here to mine it.'

A little further on Roddy drew my attention to a hillock on the southern side of the Chip Chap.

'There's about four soldiers on the top of that one. Probably overseeing the escort service.'

It gave me an uncomfortable feeling to have become the centre of a minor covert operation. I walked on, chatting to Errol as I went.

'What do you think?' I asked him.

'What do *you* think?'

A dull beat drew our attention down-valley and across the peerless blue sky came a large helicopter. It flew low over Gapshan and banked steeply above the Shyok River flats. We had come to what was ostensibly one of the loneliest spots on earth and we were being monitored every step of the way.

Out on to the vast river flats we went, the surface varying from firm shingle to diabolical quicksands. At this point the last soldier turned back. He made an obsequious farewell to Prem, giving him his escort rations of chapatti and chilli, before hurrying back towards Gapshan.

Our spirits revived. The broad, brown Depsang Plains filled the eastern horizon and downriver long red tallus slopes led the eye to white peaks that pierced the sky with their sharp summits. Disappearing into these mountains flowed the Shyok River, descending into the Shyok Gorge and eventually reaching Saser Brangsa. In a month's time we planned to take our inflatable rafts down this route and judging by the amount of water in the river at present this would be fantastic fun. A large platform extended on to the river flat; this was Gapshan grazing ground, it was well covered in grass and had been used by the yaks, ponies and camels in the bygone trading days of the Silk Road. But my thoughts were for the mountain now and looking up ahead

I could see parts of the Rimo Massif and the snouts of the Rimo Glaciers.

Two hours of marching across the vast river flats brought us to a round rock outcrop that protruded from the true left side of the flats. We stopped to have some lunch and to shelter from the unremitting blast of the north-west wind that had made each step across the waterlogged flats a battle.

From the shelter of the peninsula we struck out towards the giant white snouts of the Central and South Rimo Glaciers. The pony wallahs led their caravan towards the Central Glacier and many of the members of the party accompanied them. Rajiv thought our best Base Camp site lay on the north side of the South Rimo Glacier where a team of Indian Army engineers had camped some years before. They had experienced terrible problems getting up the glacier that way and their Base Camp had been a very long way from the foot of the mountain itself. Perhaps there would be no alternative, but recreating their difficulties did not seem prudent until we had exhausted other possibilities. So Prem and I set off towards the southern side of the South Rimo Glacier where we had both seen what appeared to be a break in the fierce defences of the glacial terminus. A stream-bed led up the side of the glacier for about a mile and above we could make out a vegetated lateral moraine platform that led even further along the glacial perimeter and thus closer to the mountain. The higher up the glacier we could get the pony caravan the less distance beyond would we have to carry our provisions. This provided us with plenty of incentive to find a good route.

We walked quickly, crossing the dozens of fast-flowing rivulets that comprised the Shyok's braided headwaters. For each crossing we followed the banks until we found a shallow rapid, generally just above a deeper chute, and here we would wade out into the freezing flow of glacial meltwater. I found my umbrella came into its own here as a walking-stick to assist with balance. On the far side we kept moving to speed circulation back into our feet and as we went our shoes squelched and spat.

Now we had to catch the others and bring them back. Climbing among the melting séracs at the glacier snout we spotted them, a string of tiny figures spread out beneath the spectacular snout of the Central Glacier. Prem's shrill whistle carried across the glacial void and eventually they rerouted themselves to join us. While Prem descended to help the caravan, I clambered across to reconnoitre the route up the glacier for the following day. It had a thick layer of moraine that was, in places, so fine it was like a sticky mud. Among the hummocks I found turquoise lakes and white granite boulders and from the top of one tall ice-ridge I managed to get the views I needed. There was good access up the stream-bed that indented the glacier's snout and above I could see a series of ramps that would probably lead us to the top of the lateral moraine wall. This would offer continuous access up the glacier for several miles and, as far as I could see, there would be a way back down on to the ice once we could go no further.

I met Prem returning. He came striding up wearing only his underpants and a parka as he had stripped off his wet gear. He was a powerful man, heavily muscled, and with a walking pace that was quick and precise. We walked beside the stream that drained this side of the South Rimo Glacier and I described what I had found. The ponies were not far behind and as they arrived the pony wallahs untied their loads, singing a soothing, murmuring folk tune to keep the animals quiet. Soon they were all unladen and standing in a quiet huddle, panting and resting. Without their loads they were diminutive creatures and few of them had any fat. The pony wallahs rounded them up and drove them to the bank of the now swollen stream. Throwing rocks and shouting they drove the ponies across, many loitering as they faltered on the unstable bottom of the stream. Some of

these exhausted animals took twenty minutes to stumble to
the far bank from where they slowly meandered their way
across half a mile of river flat to a thinly vegetated mountainside. One poor beast did not have the strength to cross the
flat and remained, pathetically, by the river all night. I did
not expect to see it alive the next morning.

Prem talked with Stopdan, one of the leading pony wallahs, about taking the caravan up the side of the glacier. To
our relief he agreed to take the animals as far as they could
safely go. I looked across the river at the frail and motionless
pony standing alone among the boulders; were we not like
slave drivers? I could not imagine that the ponies which had
reached the mountainside would succeed in getting more
than a snack from its hungry flanks. And the others? Would
they have the strength at all? I suppose I had something to
learn about the fortitude of both the people and the animals
that inhabit these mountains, for what they lack in obvious
muscle bulk they make up for with fibre, a blend of stoicism
and courage.

The majority of the Indian members had arrived and were
cheerfully putting up their tents and helping around the
camp. It did not take long for our mobile township to be
erected: Prem's tent, the cook shelter, the pony wallah tent,
stockpiles of our equipment and the tents of various members
and groups. Most of the foreign members seemed to prefer
to sleep alone, with the exception of Terry and Dave who
made it quite clear that they preferred to share their tents
with Miriam and Renée, while the Indian members preferred
a greater degree of communalism. They certainly created
some most convivial atmospheres in their tents and we all
found we migrated to one or another when we needed
company. Having put my tent up I asked Prem what had
become of the others. It appeared that PV would not cross
the now swollen river.

Two hours later people started arriving in dribs and drabs,
all of them looking wet and cold.

'That river, lad, was up to our waists,' declared Dave. 'It was more than hygienic, it was quite sterilising!'

'What happened?'

They had crossed the river in groups, forming stable lines to assist one another in the swift waters. Each group tried to convince PV to ford the river with them but to no avail. He had stripped down to his underwear in anticipation of the event but had balked each time and finally walked off up the banks of the river to the ice-cliffs of the Central Rimo Glacier which he found even more overwhelming. Eventually the combined muscle-power of Shashank, Magan and Roddy got him across. Magan told me PV's feet never touched the bottom. He stepped ashore on the west bank and giggled nervously. So nearly three hours after camp had been established we were all ensconced within its nylon walls, sipping tea and laughing about the antics of the day.

As the light began to fade Prem, Stopdan, Terry and I scrambled up on to the glacier to confirm the way ahead. Before we turned back to camp the veil of cloud that filled the upper glacier drifted south and there was our mountain. A great white pyramid, streaked with steep rock spurs and reeking of geographic defiance at the puny efforts of people such as ourselves. The few photographs that we had of this great peak had not sufficiently conveyed its scale and more than ever I knew we would have our hands full dealing with this splendid mountain. It was far steeper and much more imposing than was conveyed by the simple black-and-white images that we had scrutinised back in Australia.

The East Face was a vast and broken glacial face flanked by two tall pillars. This chaotic wall was topped by a fluted face that barred the way to the corniced summit ridge. On the south side stood the narrow niche of Ibex Col with the difficult rock buttresses of the South Face plunging down upon it. The massif sat besieged by a sea of white glacial ice divided by the elegant lines of medial moraines that converged and bifurcated during their passage down-valley.

Rimo was a magnificent objective and as I scanned its vast bulk I looked forward to the task of climbing it.

'So often it looked as if we weren't going to get anywhere near this place,' Terry said with wonder.

'And all the time spent getting here makes it even more incredible,' added Skip with a grin. 'It's great to be here.'

Skip, Terry and I wandered over to contemplate the river and assess our chances of rafting it on the return trip. Skip was the expert in this department.

'As far as I know, there is nowhere else in the world where we could be considering putting our rafts in a river at 16,000 feet and having a really good run of it.'

We stood around gloating at the variety of the fun to come and the extraordinary scenery through which we would be passing, then set off to follow Prem, Tara and Magan up the lateral moraine towards our hoped-for Base Camp site. Fingers of alpine vegetation extended into this glacial world and I revelled in the scent of alpine herbs, the subtle loveliness of the miniature blooms and the graceful folds of the lofty moraine platforms along which we marched.

Gradually the lateral moraine narrowed until the platforms petered out altogether, leaving only steep slides of moraine ahead. To my amazement the pony wallahs led the heavily laden horses down these forty-five-degree screes to the glacier 400 feet below. By the time they had all reached the ice there remained an excellent path on the moraine wall as a benefit of their passage. Such agility had always been associated with goats in my mind, not horses, and so I was further impressed with their adaptability.

A deep trough lay at the base of the moraine wall with the glacier ice crowding in on the other side. We followed this for a mile to where a glacier spilled out of a mountainside, not unlike one of those Mick Jagger tongues, and at the foot of this glacial spill-way was a perfect Base Camp site. It was flat, there was a stream filled with clear meltwater nearby and there were ridges of moraine rubble on the glacier side of the platform to protect our tents from the full onslaught of any storms and the daily catabatic winds.

There was a mixture of elation at reaching our Base Camp site and sadness as the pony wallahs untied the loads for the last time. The caravan had become a way of life over the past few weeks and I would now miss the familiar sound of the pony wallahs' singing as they removed the loads from the simple wooden harnesses and allowed the ponies to stand peacefully together, resigned to whatever might come next. With the equipment piled high around the camp we began to pay off the pony men. One by one their names were called by Wangchuk and PV and Terry counted out their wages and handed them over. They were being paid thirty-five rupees per day per pony and from the smiles and nods they all seemed pleased with their income. Roddy emptied some of the plastic barrels we had used to transport the food and gave one to each of the men which broadened their smiles further. They came round shaking us all by the hand, warm two-handed shakes, and after making a respectful farewell to Prem they turned and set off down the glacier. Stopdan was still running about the camp collecting last-minute letters for the outside world to which I contributed. Then he sprinted in pursuit of the caravan and we watched them winding their way up the moraine wall. The jangle of the horses' bells slowly diminished and we found ourselves submerged in the silence of the mountains.

The day's march had been a great help as we had covered five miles and in doing so had bypassed most of the worst séracs and moraines of the lower glacier. I climbed on to one of the ridges that overlooked the glacier and looked out over the chaos of splintered ice, water-worn runnels and teetering boulders. Beyond I could still see the colossal ice penguins of the Central Rimo Glacier hemmed in by brown mountainsides and to the west lay Mount Rimo, a giant pyramid with a pall of cloud over the summit making it look menacing and unreachable.

The afternoon was spent excavating platforms and conducting earthworks in order to create a level surface on which to pitch our tents. JP and Roddy moved hundreds of kilos of sand from near the stream to make a smooth surface void of sharp body-bruising rocks. They were very proud of this engineering feat as they collected sand and removed rocks to an appropriate rhythm that was generously pumped out by Roddy's stereo speakers.

My tent was nestled in a hollow with rock walls built around it to afford extra shelter. I put a hessian sack in front of the entrance as a doormat and spread a Kashmiri felted wool carpet on the floor; the same mat that our sable German Shepherd enjoys today in Australia. A large flat rock served as a bedside table for candles and books. Magan and Rajiv were busy building a Hindu temple by their tent and a pathway complete with stepping-stones, a massive flag of white granite for the doorstep and a line of bamboo poles with orange Grindlay's Bank marker flags adorning them. We all helped erect the dome tent in the centre of the camp, a grand yellow hemisphere with a topknot vent which looked as if it had just landed. We allotted areas for collecting drinking water, washing, toilet and rubbish incineration and Terry and I raised the expedition banner on the moraine above the camp.

When we sat around inside the dome that night everyone was smiling, smiling at having achieved the impossible. Against all the odds we had reached Base Camp and now we had to climb our mountain.

PART TWO

THE MOUNTAIN

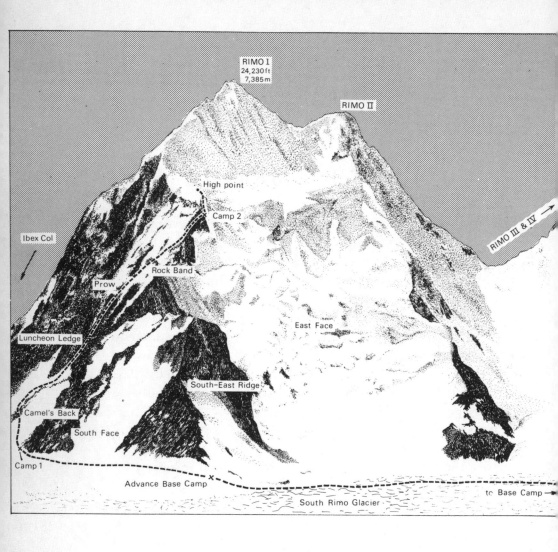

RIMO I
24,230 ft
7,385 m

RIMO II

High point

Camp 2

Ibex Col

Rock Band

RIMO III & IV

Prow

East Face

Luncheon Ledge

South-East Ridge

Camel's Back

South Face

Camp 1

Advance Base Camp

to Base Camp

South Rimo Glacier

Selecting a Line
31 August – 4 September

Six of us set out next morning on our first sortie beyond Base Camp. The route led along an arm of moraine that extended up the true right of the glacier and after several miles turned south into the Shelkar Glacier that joined the South Rimo. At this point we left the roller-coaster route through the corrugated moraines and turned out on to the ice towards Rimo. Two hundred yards out we struck what was later to be called the Mississippi: a three-metre-deep slot cut in the ice by the frictionless passage of a torrent of glacial meltwater. We could find no way round the serpentine course of this ice-ravine and so we set out to cross it. Tara cut bucket steps out to the lip of the slot and then Prem chopped a series of holes down the wall from where we were able to bridge across the torrent to the far side. With several hundred icy gallons streaming beneath your splayed legs you become acutely aware of the need to get good purchase with the pick of the ice-axe. Hauling vigorously on the axe we extricated ourselves from the Mississippi trench and continued out across the ice towards Mount Rimo.

We were moving well, certainly better than we had anticipated. Some of the stories we had been told had indicated the need for aluminium ladders to cross crevasses and terrible séracs but we were making good progress without these cumbersome tools. Just as I was on the verge of an unprecedented bout of self-congratulation over our impeccable route-finding my foot broke through a crust of ice. Automatically I spread my arms and threw myself forward to avoid going right into what I presumed was a crevasse. Splash! My foot stopped at the bottom of a pot-hole filled with water and I felt the icy cold flowing into my shoes and soaking into my socks and trousers. Recovering my dripping foot from the booby-trap, I stepped forward only to hear the same telltale 'crunch' as a boot disappeared into another. I had just been introduced to the questionable pleasure of Rimo Glacier 'pot-holing' which was to become one of the banes of crossing the glacier. No matter how careful you were, these sinister cryoconite holes got you in the end.

Southerly storms drifted in from the Shelkar range, but we were spared most of these as a window of blue sky followed us up the glacier while all around meteorological inclemency prevailed. A large mushroom cloud squatted over Base Camp dumping snow. Intermittent banks of cloud and snow engulfed Rimo and the upper glacier so that at times it felt as if we were trekking into a white void.

Four or five miles of glacier travel, periodically crossing the spine of a line of worn-down séracs and shallow crevasses, infinite numbers of the accursed pot-holes and miles of gently ascending terrain, brought us to a medial moraine. We followed this line of rocks to a cluster of granite boulders where we halted. This was an easily recognisable spot in the middle of a great expanse of nothingness. Here we left the provisions, making some rock cairns and placing flags to aid relocation. We were able to triangulate the position at the intersection of lines drawn from the East Ridge of Rimo, a small glacier that bulged out from a group of jet-black hills on the north side of the Rimo Glacier and a set of red bluffs on the south side. We had reached an altitude of 17,500 feet (5310 metres) and our spirits were similarly high. Prem sang in a lilting tenor to the mountains around us as we began the return journey down the glacier. Despite the many bamboo marker poles and orange flags with which we had flashed the route, we failed to locate one of them on that vast sea of ice. Until we established a track later in the expedition each person each time upon the glacier forged a first! It took us about two and a half hours to return to Base Camp, jumping the swollen glacier streams and dunking our feet in the pot-holes and sliding on the loose moraines.

We found that the others had nearly finished a magnificent walled structure that, although designated the kitchen tent, could also have served as a bomb shelter, such was the size of its rock walls. Renée and Miriam had sorted through the expedition food stocks and the medical gear and had made up packs of high-altitude food ready to be carried up the glacier.

We talked about the various routes we could take on the mountain and agreed only that there was no route which represented a straightforward way to the summit. We wanted to find a route that would ultimately allow most of the team to have a chance of summitting which, in retrospect, was a mistake. Rimo is a difficult mountain with no easy break in its considerable defences and, as such, was not a feasible objective for all the members of the expedition. I favoured crossing the Ibex Col and trying to finish the British route on the South Wall on the Terong-Glacier side of the col attempted by Stephen Venables and Tony Saunders in 1985. This would entail a long march – Mao would be proud of us – to reach the foot of the route and from a logistical point of view an alpine-style climb would be the only option. This approach, however, would deny many of the team the chance to attempt the mountain, as there would be no fixed ropes. Prem was determined that there should be fixed ropes and Magan was amazed that I was suggesting a climb without them. This conflict of climbing styles was complicated by the politics of international expeditioning and the limited time we had available, particularly for a conventional, fixed-rope/large-logistics approach to climbing the mountain. Compromise was to be the name of the game and, as is so often the case with compromise, it is seldom as satisfactory as a clear-cut decision.

Next day the mountain was very clear, so we were able to spend a lot of time scanning its flanks with binoculars and telephoto lenses, looking for signs of danger, such as avalanche debris, and trying to assess the best line to the summit. Prem had decided on the East Face, a glacial route up the centre of the mountain that Roddy pointed out was threatened by avalanche activity. Above this rose the 1500-foot-high fluted head wall that barred access to the summit from the east unless we could find our way along the ridges on either side. The northern of these two ridges was double-corniced and so it received an unequivocal 'no', while the ridge on the southern skyline showed some potential.

We decided that Roddy, Rajiv and I would go on a re-connaissance trip the next day, accompanied as far as the gear dump by Prem, Shashank and Tara. The idea was to be away for a few days and to reach Ibex Col from where we could evaluate the various route possibilities.

Staggering under the weight of my twenty-five-kilo load and encumbered with my skis, I was not exactly looking forward to renewing grappling contact with the Mississippi. I searched for our previous crossing spot without success and had to commit myself to a difficult climb into the slick-sided luge runnel, largely achieved by touch as I felt across the ice-wall with the tips of my toes to locate the critical ledge and allow my weight to come slowly to bear on it. I certainly couldn't see where I was putting my foot. Trapped beneath the weight of my pack, standing on a ledge large enough for one foot only and with a torrent of water rushing past the heels of my shoes I wondered if I had thought out the manoeuvre sufficiently. I knew that I could not climb the eight-foot bank on the other side with my pack on my back, so with great care I began to remove it. The twenty-five kilos swung down off my right shoulder causing me to rotate on the one foot that had a grip on something solid, albeit icy. The impartial stream at my feet continued to beckon for my pack and it occurred to me that if I dropped it it would descend unobstructed into the bowels of the glacier and my equipment would become an archaeological specimen for some future generation of scientists or booty of the military guarding this area during the next century.

Stepping across the fast-flowing water I bridged the stream and, with a grunt that could have been mistaken for an ancient mantra or a modern curse, heaved the pack above my head and on to the side of the glacier. It would not hold there and kept sliding back towards the runnel, so with one hand supporting it and the other clutching at frozen granules of ice I clawed my way up the bank to lie panting beside it. And we hadn't reached the foot of our mountain yet. To add insult to injury, I proceeded to get myself lost on the moraine and overshot the gear dump. There was no sign of Roddy, Prem, Tara, Wangchuk, Shashank or Rajiv. I called out repeatedly, 'Hello, hello!' Nothing. Finally a faint cry broke the stillness of the glacier. Back on the moraine that I had crossed was a minuscule figure waving an orange flag. He was about half a mile away and the broad sweeping waves of his arm made me think of Stevie Smith's poem, 'Not waving but drowning'. It had a humorous absurdity to it, I told myself wryly as I began to recross the malevolent stretch of glacier that separated us.

Rajiv greeted me with a smile and we began making a cup of tea. Prem and the others had returned down the glacier after dumping their loads and I could see them, a line of black dots that bobbed about on a glaring white sheet of ice.

A huge load of equipment moved steadily up through the ice and rocks below the dump. Beneath it was Roddy and he accepted a cup of tea with the alacrity of a man who needs to sip from the elixir of life lest his pack should suck it from him. I knew the problem well.

'Look out!'

Crash!

A large rock that sheltered the stove from the wind and beside which Rajiv was crouched slid off its ice-pillar and on to some of our pots.

'Someone has got it in for those pots.' The same set of pots had suffered a shocking accident at Sasoma when the truck-driver failed to locate the brake pedal and his vehicle rolled back on to a pile of our mountain kitchenware.

After spending almost an hour panel-beating some terminally dented cooking pots and sorting our gear for the carry further up the glacier, the three of us departed. By the time I had added a tent and some food to my pack it weighed the rather silly amount of thirty-five kilos. With legs bending and lungs heaving, I was embarrassed after five or ten minutes to find myself enjoying this masochistic march, head down in the mandatory coolie posture.

The moraine was fairly narrow, almost like a footpath in places with a fine gravel spread on the glacier ice. Periodically we passed large lonesome boulders that I used as progress markers as the massive scale of the glacier tended to reduce our efforts to insignificance. We crossed glacier streams that plunged into abysmal grottoes within the glacier and everywhere I found that the glacier ice itself was covered in meltwater. We had covered another three miles and were now near the base of the South-East Ridge where we had planned to establish Advance Base Camp. But where? The place was saturated and we needed somewhere dry.

A rock the size of a two-storeyed building solved the problem for it was surrounded by ice-hummocks. We shaved the crest off one of these, producing a raised platform on which to pitch our tent. The rock would provide shelter should an avalanche come off Rimo's East Face sending a wind blast capable of flattening a tent. There was plenty of water and, best of all, we would get early morning sunshine, straight from the edge of the Depsang.

The views were magnificent, down the broad sweep of the glacier with the dark lines of the medial moraines elongating what was already quite long enough. To the south lay some black hills, tiger-striped by golden strata, and high on these sensational walls were perched residual lumps of ice that were once great glaciers. Down-valley the Depsang blushed a mauve brown and the Chinese peaks beyond rose honey toned in the alpenglow. Beams of light extended from behind Rimo flooding a limelight on some of the mountains framed by the picture window of our tent and directly abeam our camp we could see the transition from the shales and sedimentary rocks of down-valley to the Karakoram granite of the Rimo Massif.

The sun had dropped into Ibex Col and with its passing came the Karakoram cold. But we were unaffected inside our sleeping bags, with the stove making that comforting roar and hot food on the boil. I looked up at the patchwork ceiling of the tent; what a veteran. It had been on two Everest expeditions before I bought it from a shrewd Tibetan in Thamel Bazaar in Kathmandu. I had used it on Makalu and Everest and, now, here it was in the Karakoram.

I zipped up the tent door, abandoning the scenery for the cosy warmth, the hum of the stove and conviviality. 'This is how I like to climb.'

'Yeh. It beats the big trips. No staff problems here.'

Mugs of tea and stewed apricots with ginger bran biscuits crumbled over them got us going next morning, sitting in our sleeping bags like partially metamorphosed larvae. Completing the transition from sedentary to upright beings we pulled on our cross-country ski boots and wriggled out of the tent.

I had been looking forward for a long time to positioning the square toe of my boots over the three pins of the ski binding, locking the bail and slipping my hands through the wrist loops of the ski poles. I was ready and exited camp, at first with a slightly stiff diagonal stride, towards the base of Rimo's South-East Ridge. To my left rose a fold of crevassed ice forming the entrance to the glacier that followed the southern flank of the mountain. I studied the broken ice for a route until I found a suitable line that snaked through the large crevasses on the crest of the slope and led on to the broad glacier above.

Setting off for the first time into an area where there are many crevasses is always a time of apprehension, intensified for me by the fact that I was alone. Rajiv and Roddy were well behind and chose to carry their skis until they were above the crevassed slope. I hurried past the dark openings fearing the silence of those icy bowels as much as their perennial patience. Where necessary I probed with my ski poles, often checking the small crevasses to make sure that that was what they were. It was like a maze where the odds were not as jocular as the funfair version, yet far more inspiring.

The smooth white of the glacier beyond beckoned and once on this cleaner surface I moved quickly. My breathing synchronised with the pace of the alternately darting skis. I gained altitude rapidly, leaving a thin white line on the snow behind. The notch of the Ibex Col grew ahead of me and the vertical expanse of the South Face of Rimo rose overhead, yielding precious few of its secrets. Eventually, I stopped abeam two slender gullies that led up the face through bands of rock to the crest of the South-East Ridge. From there we would have to follow the serrated cornices of the ridge itself to the summit. The route looked feasible, although it had some very exposed sections towards the top which would prove difficult for a tired party and in bad weather.

Two tiny figures moved up the glacier and joined me opposite these gullies.

'They look like good routes. But we need to know what happens at the top where they join the ridge,' Roddy mumbled with food in his mouth and Terry's monocular binoculars to his right eye.

'Those rock bands will be steep but otherwise they look okay. I think the left one is the best,' I added. 'It'll put us higher on the ridge and, hopefully, beyond the gendarmes we saw from Advance Base.'

'Yeh. That looks the go. The ridge above that is pretty straightforward until it reaches that step above the plateau on the East Face. There are some really big cornices, but I think we can go round the back of them. Have a look, Rajiv.' Roddy passed the monocular binoculars.

Rajiv was an extraordinarily fit and agile man, very slight and with keen dark eyes that seemed to flash with the intensity of each precise movement. I felt sure that he would have already seen the route but he took the binoculars and scanned the mountain that filled the northern sky above us.

'It is possible,' he said after a pause. 'I think we can climb this way.' He made a sweeping gesture that covered the field of vision.

'I would like to see the British route,' I said. 'I still think that it is the best bet. Shall we try to reach the Ibex Col?'

A piercingly cold wind off the col made movement of any kind welcome, even upward. The snow thinned and progressively we were forced to ski on sheets of green ice peppered with shards of rock. This made it difficult, if not impossible, for our skis to hold and progress slowed to a frustrating series of slides and scrambles.

Pillars rose from the col in foreshortened profusion and they were separated by gullies that acted as spill-ways for tenuous ice-cliffs high on the mountain; and so another series of route possibilities bit the proverbial dust. To my dismay the Ibex Col was also a sheet of ice and at forty-five degrees quite beyond my cross-country skis.

'Looks too steep without crampons, Rajiv.'

'The only way for us is the gully we saw below,' he replied. 'Anyway, Colonel wants to climb on this side of the col. Over there it will be too far. Many of the members will not even get to the bottom!' He smiled.

'Shall we try to get a little closer?' I urged. 'Whatever we do let's keep moving because I don't like the look of those ice-cliffs.'

A strong blast of cold wind whipped down the wall of the col stinging our faces with chips of ice. The decision was made. We began to descend from our high point directly beneath the col at 19,500 feet (5930 metres) to where Roddy had stopped a short way below. The wind-rutted snow and the sheets of slick ice made for some interesting telemarking. It was at this point that I was reminded that Rajiv had never skied on cross-country skis before. Poor fellow; what a place to learn.

Roddy and I skied down avoiding the ice wherever possible and just hanging in there when we couldn't. Near the spot where we had had lunch we sped through several acres of avalanche debris, which emphasised the transience of all things and encouraged us to seek the fall line and go faster. Periodically we stopped to scrutinise the South Face and the gully route. From every aspect it looked a reasonable route for our team's capabilities. During these spells for observation we were also treated to the spectacle of Rajiv's determined descent from the col. A tiny figure repeatedly moved out across the white ice, gaining speed until, in a flurry of rotating arms and legs and skis and poles, he would disappear into a snow-coated heap. These meteoric terminations came to represent the point where Rajiv stoically turned his skis for a schuss in the opposite direction. Trying to emulate a long fast schuss Roddy and I had made from one side of the glacier to the other, the heroic Rajiv gained speed as he pointed his skis into the bowl beneath him. But his tuck slipped back into a rear-weighted squat which deposited him on the back of his skis just as he flew into wind-crusted snow. Rajiv exploded and out of the cloud of snow emerged a bedraggled figure carrying his skis. It was infuriating for someone who

Everybody liked Jonga. We just wished he could cook.

Stopdan and some of the pony wallahs consumer testing Peter's stereo equipment.

Six heads are wiser than one: Shashank, Rajiv, Magan, Skip, Brett and Peter at Advance Base.

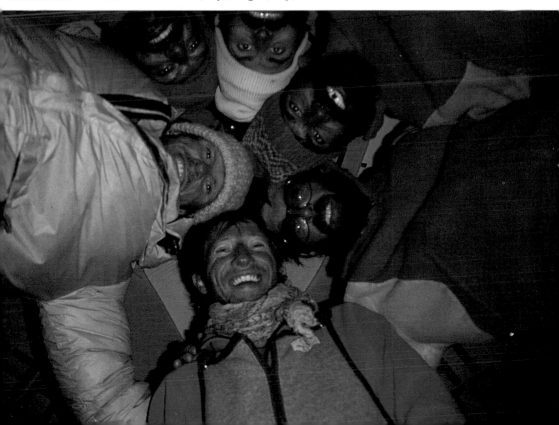

Camp 1, Seacliffs, at the foot of the South Face, with Skip in the foreground.

Rajiv, determined on skinny skis near Camp 1.

A lone figure ascends the South Face beneath granite spires.

Above Camp 1: above left, Skip leads the first pitch above the Camel's Back. Note where the avalanche broke away. Above right, Skip leads the ice pitch below the Rock Band. Below left, Skip on the Rock Band. Below right, Magan ascending the fixed rope above the Rock Band.

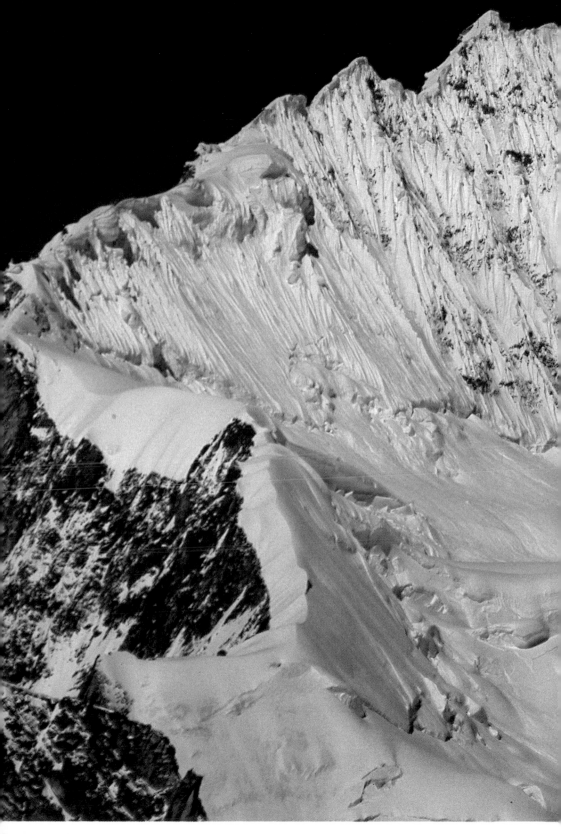

A view up the South-East Ridge.

The Siachen peaks as seen from Camp 2.

Looking back over the South Rimo Glacier to the Depsang Plains from 22,000 feet.

Above Camp 2 at 22,000 feet on the South-East Ridge: above, Skip and Roddy; below left, Roddy and Magan; below right, Skip and Roddy sort out ropes before our last pitch on Rimo.

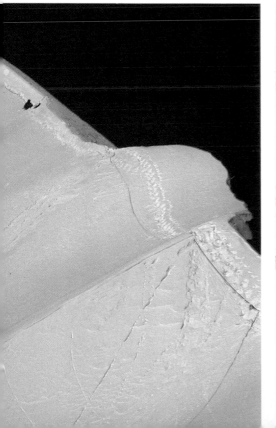

Turning our backs on Rimo we set out from Base Camp to Sasoma weighed down by our forty-six-kilo packs.

Dave, Skip, Terry and Peter grind to a halt at the avalanche below the Khardung La.

is such a good downhill skier, but cross-country skiing is different and the conditions were abominable.

Before returning to Advance Base we skied south into a tributary glacier to get a better perspective of the southern aspects of the mountain and in particular the summit ridge. The South-East Ridge looked distinctly promising from this more distant angle, and we set off down towards camp feeling convinced that we had identified a reasonable route on the east side of Ibex Col.

Next morning a short walk north of camp gave us a better view of the East Face of Rimo and another aspect of the South-East Ridge. The lower part of the ridge was very steep and this confirmed our decision to take the left of the two South Face gullies as it would top out above the more difficult terrain. The East Face certainly was a possibility but the avalanche and sérac danger was considerable and once one had reached the plateau beneath the summit pyramid the route would have to join the South-East Ridge. We concluded that the gully route to the ridge and then the ridge to the summit was our best bet on this side of the mountain and with that we began retracing our steps down the medial moraine towards the gear dump.

The recce had bred a camaraderie in our party which had been missing during our earlier piecemeal progress. Now we had a feeling of achievement and looked forward to the progress we should make on the mountain.

8

Bad Weather Blues
4 – 15 September

At the gear dump we got on with that most civilised of tasks, boiling the billy and making tea, and we were able to extend the civilities of a nice cuppa to Prem, Shashank, Dave and Tara when they arrived en route to stock Advance Base. It was our turn for a rest day at Base Camp.

'You should hurry down,' said Tara with a mischievous smile. 'Jonga is cooking something special.'

'I'll stay here,' we replied as one man.

Every time Jonga's culinary skills came up I found myself thinking of Pong, the infamous cook in W. E. Bowman's *The Ascent of Rum Doodle*. But that was a light-hearted skit on climbing expedition life. Jonga was for real and guaranteed to turn any ingredient into glue. When Magan had offered to show him how to cook rice Jonga had ordered him from the tent, declaring that his credentials as an expedition cook were superior to Magan's and that he needed no coaching from him. Apart from Jonga's erroneous belief in his ability to create food that was not a crime against humanity, he was a pleasant enough fellow although I doubt some of us will ever forgive him for his most vile victuals.

For three hours we crossed the glacier, its streams and Mississippis, its pot-holes and séracs and, finally, the agonising moraine that led us down the southern side of the glacier to Base Camp.

Cups of tea delivered by 'tea please' Dorje, our cookboy, and the comfortable familiarity of our tents was a welcome relief from the rigours up-valley; that was until dinner-time when I dreamed about the relative luxury of our evening repasts at Advance Base as I chewed my way through Jonga's latest outrage to the culinary art. When the food was as repulsive as this one had plenty of time to look around at one's companions, who seemed to be doing much the same. Mouths full, chewing slowly on some indestructible lump in the dhal, our gazes drifted around the tent. Everyone had established a spot for themselves in the mess tent to which they returned every meal-time and these positions appeared to be part of the group dynamics. Skip always sat near the door, whereas Magan and PV always sat near Prem; Dave, Renée, JP and I always sat opposite the door and the others always sat opposite Prem. By now, too, I had worked out which members of the party would co-operate unquestioningly with the decision-makers and who would not; those who felt responsible for the actions of the expedition as a whole and those who did not.

To be woken next morning by a manifestation of group dynamics in discord was something else.

A voice bellowed out. It was Roddy and it sounded as if he did not have JP's best interests at heart. They had not been getting on during the past couple of days and the combination of JP's often headstrong ways and Roddy's own strengths was putting amicability to the test. I looked out of my tent, a real 'sticky-beak' neighbour, and watched the furore. JP's turbaned head jerked about as he remonstrated with Roddy. Out of the corner of my eye I saw someone coming; it was Magan, back from doing his morning puja with a red tika on his forehead. His flourishing beard bristled and his hair waved behind him as he strode briskly up to fix Roddy with an icy stare.

'Is he your servant?' he demanded.

'What?!' responded a perplexed Mackenzie.

'Is he your servant?'

'No.'

'If he is not your servant, then please do not speak to him that way!'

A hush fell over the camp.

Terry, Magan and Skip departed up the glacier to join Prem, Shashank, Dave and Tara at our Advance Base. They were going to assist with ferrying loads from the dump and later would move ahead to establish a camp at the base of the route. They would begin work on the climb as soon as possible. The dreaded Jonga, Dorje and Errol were going to carry a load to the dump and would return to Base Camp later in the afternoon. Jonga's absence enabled Miriam and Renée to invade the sordid kitchen area and produce a delicious luncheon of fish, potato chips, bread and spreads, custard and mango slices and rich chocolate drinks. We all needed a siesta after such a meal before continuing with the task of making up loads of provisions for the camps up the glacier and on the mountain. Roddy's and my stereo speakers thumped out a background beat. Throwing in a 'craw, craw' every so often were a few black ravens perched on the moraine wall above camp. Otherwise we were left to ourselves.

Late in the afternoon PV and Wangchuk arrived back from the Gepshan army camp where they had gone to try to send messages about extending our permit. PV was looking rather pleased with himself so I assumed he had been received warmly this time.

'How did it go, PV?'

'Oh, it was very fine. The camp commander is very sorry that he was not able to be hospitable to us. He sends his apology to Colonel also. We had some very good food.' PV was also looking rather spruce.

'Did you have a hot wash down there too?' I asked a little jealously.

'Yes, I was having the hot shower. The army has all the facilities.'

'Lucky you. Any news from Delhi?'

'No messages for us. They are not receiving any communications. Their radio is not working.'

'Can you reach Leh with your radio?'

'No, it is not possible. It is for short range only. Now the battery is flat also.' He looked stern.

What to do? Restoring PV's *amour propre* was one thing, but not as high on our list of priorities as getting an extension to our permit.

That evening I wandered along the moraine wall above camp as the sun sank into the trough of Ibex Col. Laughter came from some tents where jokes were being told, elsewhere cards were being played and the silence from other tents told of the occupants' concentration on what they were reading or writing. Roddy's stereo was playing some Hindi songs. The high-pitched female voice of the soloist carried into the air above the camp and I heard a muffled comment drift from Brett's tent to Miriam's.

'Bloody cat music. It's like a whining cat.'

Forty-two days had passed since I left home and we were only now beginning to come to grips with the mountain. Sometimes I wondered if this journey would ever end and whether I'd ever get to see Ann again. Without any communication or mail from the outside world one can feel very out of touch. We had become all the more attuned to the All India news on the radio. Any news was better than no news to a clan of media-dependent members of the twentieth century, even if it was about hijacks in the Middle East, terrorism in Europe, famine in Africa, the President of the United States banging on about the 'evil empire of the USSR' and floods on the Gangetic Plains. To a tiny encampment in a mountain desert in Central Asia the news of the world becomes a vicarious pleasure akin to eavesdropping, a source of gossip to be bandied about over breakfast. It provided a social safety valve for there are few safer topics for discussion than events in the far-flung corners of the world; particularly if you reside in the Eastern Karakoram, itself the epitome of far flung.

Our next sortie to the dump was delayed by six inches of snowfall overnight which would have made the moraines treacherous. But by lunch-time the cloud had burned off, the famous 'blue skies of Ladakh' returned and we were treated to the harsh glare of sun and snow.

Jonga's travesty of lunch was thankfully interrupted by the arrival of Prem and Shashank from Advance Base Camp.

'So much snow,' sighed Prem. 'The others are going up the glacier from Advance Base to establish the Camp 1 either today or tomorrow. Terry and Skip have been ill but they are much better now. We thought we would see you on the glacier?'

We all looked a little sheepish and quickly offered Prem some lunch. It was dahl bhat with an unspeakable sauce.

Prem sat himself on a large rock near his tent and unlaced his boots. His feet were wet and shrivelled by hours of glacial pot-holing and he let the warm sun dry them.

'We've carried many shuttles between Advance Base and the dump. Now there is very little left there. The ravens broke into some of our tsampa so we need more of that. And JP! Those cans of fruit juices are still at the dump. If I had not been so tired I would have brought them back down.'

JP loved his tinned fruit juices and considered them as essential rations. But now that the ponies had left and we were the coolies such heavy foods went out of favour for anywhere but Base Camp. JP took it all in good humour, a broad smile creasing his bearded face.

'Tomorrow Roddy, Rajiv and Peter should go up to Advance Base to join Magan, Dave, Tara, Skip and Terry. You can support them by carrying loads to the Camp 1 while they begin to fix the route. Then you can take over to finish fixing the ropes to the ridge-line at the top of the South Face. What do you think?' Prem asked.

'Sounds good to me. From the ridge we will have to climb without fixed ropes as we won't have much left by then. In any case there won't be time to fix any further. We could set up a relay system on the ridge so that teams can share equipment above the fixed ropes.'

'Yes, that should be all right.' Prem nodded.

A blur of letter-writing consumed what was left of another restful day. Later in the evening cloud rolled down the valley and engulfed us in a veil of sleet. I pulled the door zipper down and looked out at the changing face of our Base Camp. The two sacks that I had laid outside as my doormat were white and so were my gym shoes, which I hurriedly gathered, slapping the soles together to shake off the snow. I shrank back into my tent and re-zipped the door. For something to do I began to tear an overdue brush through the snarled and knotted tangles of my hair, peering at my unfamiliar reflection in a small hand mirror. A bristle that would soon qualify as a beard encrusted my face and so did a matrix of crazed lines. I spied a few grey hairs and concluded that the rigours of age and expeditions were taking their toll. A British Columbian health farm was my only hope! I analysed the symptoms of decay with a certain morbidity as I applied some moisturising cream. While I massaged this white elixir into my skin I read the small print: 'You too can look more beautiful'!

This encouraging discovery was interrupted by the sound of Dorje beating a pot lid down by the cook shelter. I risked pneumonia by going outside, gastro-enteritis if I made it through a plate of Jonga's poison.

Brett and I filmed our departure from camp next day and the large party winding its way through the moraine above. There were the predictable antics involved in crossing the Mississippi, human chains tugging one another over the channel and the nine of us meandering through the penguins, those ghostly effigies of once-proud séracs. We ploughed on across the disheartening plain of pot-holes to arrive with some relief at the gear dump where we threw ourselves down on our packs for a brief spell of r and r. Most of the others left their loads and started back to Base Camp, while Roddy, Renée, Rajiv and I remained for an extended intermission before we topped up our loads to over thirty kilos and staggered on towards Advance Base.

The strain of carrying such large loads twelve miles up the glacier focused my thoughts on the problem we had with supplying the camps up there. Of course nearly everybody wanted to get to Advance Base, but the more people who stayed there, the more quickly our resources would be drained. Precedence must be given to the strongest climbers and to those actively involved on the hill. This was the conviction of all the stronger climbers but it was less vigorously adopted by the rest. A typical scenario of political expediency.

An hour later we reached Advance Base. The yellow dome was now pitched here and made a most welcome sight as we walked into the tight cluster of tents. Tara greeted us with mugs of soup and rushed out of camp to take Renée's pack for the last hundred yards.

'Magan, Skip, Terry and Dave have gone up this morning. I have been here alone. It has been a nice day,' Tara said. He had a handsome smile and as he stood there in front of his newly constructed cook shelter, I observed that he would surely win the best-dressed-climber-on-the-expedition award – grey European woollen britches, long patterned Austrian socks, a cream shirt cut large and comfortable with plenty of gussets, and a blue scarf casually knotted about his neck. 'Why don't you put your things in the big tent? I and Colonel are using that one.' He pointed to one of our climbing tents pitched beside the giant boulder. 'I can bring the dinner to you up there, okay?'

'That would be great. What are the others doing today?'

'We found a very good site for Camp 1 two days ago. They will put the camp there today and maybe start work on the climb also. Tomorrow you can all carry food up to them.'

The thought of carrying anything at that moment did not do much for me nor for my sore shoulders. I picked up my pack and followed Roddy and Renée to the dome tent where we passed the evening talking about our families, eventually agreeing that it was the nature of families to be eccentric. One day, perhaps, we would meet a family that was certified 'normal', but we couldn't imagine where.

Rajiv and Tara descended the medial moraine to the gear dump to ferry a load back to Advance Base and Roddy and I put on our skis and carried some tents, ropes and fuel up to Camp 1. We followed the route we had used before, although most signs of our passage had disappeared beneath wind-blown spindrift. The undulations of the glacier terminated at the base of the South-East Ridge where it climbed more steeply through the crevasses and out on to the cwm that leads to the Ibex Col. The sun got hotter as the day wore on and the wet snow began to ball up on the undersides of our skis.

I found Camp 1 in an idyllic wind hole beneath a golden outcrop that jutted out from the flanks of the South-East Ridge. The Northstar tent was pitched between the granite and the vertical wall of ice that formed the side of the wind scoop. It was like a frozen wave pounding a rocky shore, a freeze frame, and so Camp 1 was called Seacliff. Behind the tent were two pools of water and around the tent were shelves of flat stone on which to cook and sit and sun oneself. The vista down the glacier to the east was breathtaking; the glacier spread before us and on the horizon was the mysterious Depsang. I could espy the vicinity of Base Camp but the great distances made identifying the actual tents impossible.

No one was at home at Seacliff, and I could not see any sign of them up on the South Face. I decided to go for a reconnaissance, but later. The reflected heat was unbearable, so I unzipped the tent and flopped inside. For an hour I lay resting, drinking from my water bottle and nibbling dried fruit and nuts. When Roddy arrived we started a stove and produced a pot of syrupy tea, pouring what remained into a water bottle before setting off to see how the climb was going.

We traversed some icy slopes towards the foot of the gullies that led up through the rock bands of the face above. Perched above a prominent hump, later to be called the Camel's Back, Roddy spotted the others. They were climbing a steep ice-pitch that led into the left-hand gully and would have been sweltering in the heat. We were both delighted to see them for at long last the climb proper had begun. It had taken one and a half months since leaving Australia for the expedition proper to begin climbing; it had to be an unenviable record.

An exhilarating twenty minutes delivered us to Advance Base from Camp 1. Skiing was unquestionably the solution to the load-carrying blues. Directing our skis down the railway tracks of our upward journey we sped down the glacier and linked turns through the exposed crevasses near the foot of the South-East Ridge. A final schuss across the rutted glacier to the Advance Base boulder and we were there.

'Hey, that looks good!' came a voice from amidst the crackling, whirring sound of radio interference. I looked up to see Rajiv and Tara who were lying in the sun and listening to the occasional audible phrase of a radio broadcast.

'It's the second one-day match.'

'Of what?' I asked.

'Cricket! India versus Australia in Bombay.'

'How outrageously incongruous . . .' The static died down suddenly and the cricket commentary continued.

'Shhhh!' commanded Tara.

'What a magnificent ball by the young Australian. Mathews

has bowled another maiden over for Australia . . .' The Bombay commentator brought back the memory of a hundred Saturdays when cricket was compulsory and I was fourteen.

A shroud of cloud hung over the massive triangle of Rimo. Ranks of pale cirrus were drifting in from the west and elsewhere the sky was clear. We retreated to our sleeping bags and into the covers of books for a candle-lit evening on the glacier.

Twelve hours of uninterrupted horizontal rest preceded the new day. Roddy, none the less, seemed loath to wake. 'If there is one thing I do well it is definitely sleeping,' he murmured from the confines of his bag. 'Yeh, I am very good at sleeping. The long nights are no problem at all. I reckon I could go on for sixteen, seventeen hours quite possibly. I don't often get the opportunity to test these theories but I'm quite sure that I could. I mean, sleeping is the next best thing to sex. It's hard to dispute it.'

After breakfast Tara and Renée descended to the dump to collect more provisions left there by Errol, Brett and Prem, while Rajiv joined Roddy and me for another carry up the glacier to Camp 1. Flurries of snow were falling, but as the cloud shifted patches of blue sky and sunshine made us sweat. As we climbed we probed the surface for crevasses, hoping to create visual warning of their whereabouts for our descent.

One hour and thirty-five minutes of diagonal stride saw us at the camp, despite the fickle weather. We chopped out a tent platform in the snow below the North Star, pitched the two-man Olympus mountain tent and pushed all the provisions we had brought with us into this, together with any gear we found lying around in the drifting snow. Then, leaving a chit for the Camp 1 team who were again out on the face fixing ropes, we departed at speed. Twenty-five minutes of partially blind descent in the wind-blown snow, jumps over small crevasses and telemarks through the broken terrain near Advance Base led us to the dome tent. Just five minutes later Tara and Renée returned with their packloads of food from the dump and we were soon all together in the dome sipping tea and taking a consumer interest in the supplies they had just brought with them.

A half-moon peered through the envelopes of grey cloud that removed all sense of location and disorientated the senses. Perhaps that was why there had been no sign of anyone from Base Camp at the dump.

'Today is JP's birthday,' announced Tara. 'They must be celebrating.'

'I wonder what that culinary maestro, Jonga, has whipped up for the troops in honour of it? What are we having, Tara?'

'Rice and green peas.' The peas were like bullets and could well have been recyclable.

A new day dawned with utter inclemency; snow fell from the bleak skies and wind blew drifts of snow around the dome. We left camp wearing our windsuits with snow blowing past us as we skiied up the glacier. It conjured images of Scott and Antarctica and as we climbed higher the weather became even more miserable, with tiny pieces of wind-blown ice stinging our faces. It became much colder and I had difficulty keeping my hands warm.

Camp 1 loomed out of the swirling whiteness of the storm. I gave a yell and a zipper slid across a wall of nylon.

'Come on in, mate,' Terry called, as Rajiv and I removed our skis and packs and wriggled into the crowded tent. 'Welcome to Seacliff.' The stove was going and it was warm and humid inside. We propped ourselves around the wall of the tent and were soon enjoying hot chocolate drinks and soup. The tales of what was happening on the mountain and down below were quickly dispensed with and we got on to speculating on Roddy's whereabouts. He had left with us.

I put on my boots and returned outside to the wind and

horizontal snow. A hundred yards from the camp I saw a dark silhouette that soon materialised into the familiar character of Mackenzie moving slowly towards me.

'What happened, Roddy?'

'I fell into a crevasse.'

'What?'

'Where?'

'Are you okay?'

'I tried to take a short-cut off your ski tracks, only a couple of yards or so, and I broke through. I fell about three yards into this bloody huge crevasse. I landed on a bridge, which didn't do my skis much good, but stopped the fall.'

'We were wondering what you were doing, lad. Glad to hear you've been having a nice time.'

'Once I had climbed out I stopped and had some lunch to give myself a rest. Any more of that soup?'

'Ych, here you go, mate.'

It was fun to have the seven of us squeezed into that small storm-encircled tent. We had not seen each other for over a week and in that time the other five had visibly changed. Tattered pieces of zinc oxide medical tape were hanging off their cracked fingers, their peeling red noses and well-tanned faces told of the long days on the face and their smiles conveyed the rest. They had fixed rope up the lower part of the South Face already.

Magan and Dave togged up and descended to Advance Base, leaving the rest of us to continue the chatter, and brew, as Roddy and Skip engaged in a protracted debate over how one should cook macaroni and a pre-cooked meal in a foil sachet.

'The water has to boil first.'

'Yes, I know. But unless we put some extra water into the pot we can't cook the two together.'

'What's that, then? Two stoves!'

'Where are we going to cook the soup? And stew the apricots?'

'Look, put the soup on this one; is it going yet?'

'Just about.'

'Do the macaroni here and we'll stew the apricots later.'

'I wasn't saying I wanted apricots with my macaroni, if that's what you're getting at. I want to have my dinner before morning.'

'Leave it to me.'

'That's what I wanted to do in the first place.'

Eventually a meal was served that was approximately *al dente*, although it did stick to the walls of the tent.

All night the wind howled and the snow battered us in violent waves.

'I think we should drink more coffee. The weather's horrible outside,' Skip declared in the morning.

'Sit tight,' Terry agreed. 'As soon as we get a clearance we can do the rest of the face in a day, say a day and a half. The weather's got to break soon,' he continued, demonstrating his infamous and untoward optimism.

'It's been doing this for two consecutive days now. Even our last day up on the mountain was pretty wild,' said Skip, slurping coffee. 'There were strong winds and spindrift pouring down the face. It was really neat being up there. Wind-eddies carrying piles of snow around, getting in your ears and freezing the ropes up. The jumars were only half hanging on to the rope. You had to keep cleaning the ice off.' He paused and listened to the wind whipping over the tent and lashing it with snow and sleet. 'I wouldn't want to be up there now, though.'

'The face is so exposed. It catches the full force of the weather,' put in Terry.

'The face could well be nothing compared with what we'll get on the ridge,' I predicted. 'Probably the best thing we can do now is to go down to conserve rations here and have a change of scene. If we can't work on the hill we might as well be elsewhere.'

'Brave those winds,' moaned Terry. 'All we need is a break. Five good days and I think we could get someone on the summit.'

'I reckon we've only had one burst of five consecutive good days in the last two months,' observed Skip, to which we reluctantly agreed.

'So much for those "blue skies of Ladakh".'

'Yeh. We've been ripped off for sure.'

'Who is the Minister of Tourism and Propaganda in this state?'

Roddy's accident made me apprehensive where before I had skied with confidence. The white-out conditions made it even more frightening so I skied fast to ensure that my velocity would carry me over any crevasses. There was a cup of hot soup in my hands just thirty minutes from leaving Camp 1; the others arrived two hours later having waded down more cautiously through fresh snow.

Magan had returned to Base Camp that morning, leaving ten of us at Advance Base waiting for fine weather. Errol and Brett had arrived and had brought my stereo speakers so that rock-'n'-roll could compete with the elements.

The pros and cons of descending to Base Camp or sitting out the storm were debated. No one was keen on going down but with ten people we only had food for three days. That evening Miriam, JP and Shashank arrived, making our party up to thirteen. Shashank brought a letter from Prem.

Terry's brow furrowed as he read it. 'I think Prem is losing interest in the climb – all the hassles we've had and now the weather. And we still don't have our permit extension. Some of us are going to have to go down to talk to him and that way we'll reduce the number of people up here, too.'

Prem's letter had simply said he was considering returning to Manali and that he wished us the best of luck on the mountain.

It was generally felt that Prem had lost heart because of the numerous problems the expedition had had, many of which he had taken very personally. I think the initial differences of opinion over the route to be attempted on Rimo had not been satisfactorily reconciled in his mind either, and as a leader used to military obedience among the expedition members he could have felt he had become superfluous. Nothing could have been further from the truth.

Terry was deputy leader and so the responsibility for sorting out the problem fell on his shoulders. The next morning Terry's normal ebullience was strained and he looked tired as he packed his things while Miriam applied a brilliant blue mascara to her eyelashes. Terry, Miriam, Dave and Renée started down the glacier, with JP and me accompanying them as far as the dump to bring a load of provisions back up to Advance Base, while all the others humped loads up to Camp 1. The weather became worse as the day went on. If there was one thing that was proceeding as predicted it was the weather forecasts.

Our world merely altered in degrees of unsullied whiteness, diluting that sense of mission that one perceives when one's objective stands more defined.

JP, Tara and I sat on cold rocks in the freezing cook shelter listening to JP's mountaineering anecdotes.

'It was an angle of sixty degrees and the ice was hard on Kamet,' he said, 'and on Brigapanth, too, and even the weather was bad but, my dear, not like this.'

'I wonder if we'll ever get to do any climbing at this rate. Here we are at the foot of one of the most superb unclimbed peaks left in the world and all Huey's doing is dumping on us.'

'What? Who's that?'

'Whoever's up there running the weather department.'

'Yes, I agree with you,' JP replied, looking down at his boots which he tapped together a few times. 'This is a very good opportunity but we are not blessed with good weather. Chai.' He reached out his cup for Tara to fill it with a thick brown liquid. Just then a gust carried snow into the shelter, turning us all into snow leopards.

Rajiv, Skip and Shashank returned. They looked elated after their wild trip up to Camp 1. There had been very strong winds and deep drifting snow but that, it seemed, had only improved the otherwise unexciting trek. On their return they met Roddy, Brett and Errol. Roddy was still not feeling well and had been moving very slowly so they had decided to cache their loads on a rock shelf below Camp 1 and begin the return journey. When Roddy did get back he looked both ill and depressed.

The storm raged on. The excess of time out from our climb was turning us sullen. Tara and Rajiv retreated early to their tent, while the ailing Mackenzie griped with Skip over some matter of consuming importance and complete incon-sequence, whereas Brett maintained a monosyllabic brevity in his communications with one and all. Fittingly, the tem-perature plummeted to nearly twenty below zero and the wind blew stiffly from the north-west which drove us to our beds early, fusing reticence with silence.

The tracks around camp, once furrows, were drifted over, returning the glacier to a state of peneplanation. Kerbs of snow had ebbed up against the tents and the entire camp bore an air of 'the morning after'. Morale was drop-ping away into an irreversible pessimism and, I think for many, thoughts of home and other places dominated their musings.

After an early lunch on 15 September, JP, Roddy and Errol descended towards Base Camp. A clearance in the early evening had the rest of us out on the glacier, cameras in hand and making all those predictable statements of awe and wonder that accompany the end of the storm and a beautiful sunset.

'Someone's coming!' I called, noticing a figure, that became two, moving steadily up the medial moraine.

'This is becoming like musical chairs. One lot goes and another comes.'

'Who is it?'

'Is it Roddy and JP coming back? They were predicting an improvement in the weather.'

'It's Colonel,' said Tara with a smile of real pleasure.

Prem and Magan marched into camp with such vigour that it was almost overwhelming. Prem had obviously decided to set things straight.

'I have told Errol and JP to work on ferrying loads to the dump. This mountain is not for them. Roddy can come back if he gets well again. There is no point in his being here when he's not well. Terry and Dave are going to do a carry to the gear dump and they will come up to Advance Base in a couple of days' time. I'm sorry there is no news about our permit extension so time is very short.'

'Any news of Jack, Prem?' asked Skip.

'Nothing. PV will try to contact Gepshan but otherwise we don't know.'

Prem drank tea in the cook shelter with Tara and Magan while the rest of us pitched a tent he had brought up with him. The weather kept improving and Prem was declared the harbinger of clear skies. With the tent erected, Skip walked over to him.

'Your tent is ready, sir.'

Prem had injected renewed vitality into the party and, while the twilight glanced its final beams upon the snow-capped Depsang, he briefed us on his plans for the morning. 'Tomorrow Magan and I will carry a load from the dump while Skip, Rajiv, Peter, Brett and Shashank should go back up to Camp 1 and start fixing the ropes. I and Magan will join you there tomorrow. How long do you think it will take you to fix ropes to the ridge?'

'A few days, all going well.'

The evening kept expanding, with Magan's booming laugh and Prem's high-pitched shriek. Our enthusiasm soared beyond the morning's doldrums and we all felt ready for the new day and a return to the mountain. Outside Rimo glowed magnificently in the moonlight.

9

To the South-East Ridge
16 – 24 September

The pale light of dawn filtered into our tents and its message was reinforced by a lion-like roar from Prem's tent. We all pushed our heads out into a peerless morning where the Depsang glowed a shimmering gold and all the peaks stood with a perfect clarity in the azure sky. Colonel Prem was already out in the chilling air encouraging us all to get moving and return to the fray and Camp 1 at Seacliff.

There were five of us, Rajiv, Shashank, Skip, Brett and I. I was the only one still trusting to skis. Near the base of the South-East Ridge I crossed one crevasse that I assumed to be more insipient than substantial and as I began my diagonal stride there was a dull thudding sound as a void appeared between my legs. My skis, like seven-foot feet, kept me perched on the rims and with some energetic pole work I completed the crossing of what was now a very large hole indeed.

At Seacliff we cut out a platform and assembled the dome tent before settling in. Later Shashank, Brett and I carried up some more loads from a dump above Advance Base, while the others prepared our gear for the morning.

When I crawled out of the tent to collect some ice for the early morning breakfast of tea and tsampa, all was quiet. The wind had abated and the sky smiled in a waxen moonlit light upon the mountains.

'Conditions couldn't be better,' I called to the others.

By 8.00 a.m. we were on our way, plugging in deep snow up the glacier to the base of our gully on the South Face, where we zigzagged up to the Camel's Back which was the outcrop where the fixed ropes began. Skip started up the rope kicking deep holes in the fresh snow until, as he approached the crest of a steep bulge in the slope, there was a 'crack' and a 'whoosh!'

The slope released with a sudden ferocity and broke up into large slabs of snow that raced off down each side of the Camel's Back. Skip had his axe in the snow above the avalanche fracture-line and below his feet kicked about in the air until he managed to find purchase on the icy surface that had just been exposed.

'Wow!' he cried out.

'How's your pulse?' Brett inquired.

The weather was perfect but the slopes would take several days to stabilise. We would have to be careful.

For several hours we 'jugged' the ropes up the gully, jumars slipping frequently on the iced ropes, until we came to a ledge where the ropes ended.

'We're at exactly 20,000 feet,' I told the others.

We were four men standing on a ledge where there was only room for one to lie down. I was preparing to take over the lead and we were all taking the opportunity to stuff some food into our mouths. This became a universal ritual when we reached this spot and so it was given the name Luncheon Ledge.

'I think Shashank has turned back.'

'I hope he's left the rope and gear up here somewhere,' said Skip.

'He should have,' answered Rajiv. 'He knows we need the rope up here.'

'One good thing is he'll have tea ready when we get back,' Brett said with a grin.

'Yeh, and Magan will probably have dinner ready too,'

enthused Skip. Since we had escaped the jurisdiction of Jonga's kitchen we were able to look forward to our food. 'He'll have a five-course dinner waiting for us!'

Skip transferred his attention to my constricted preparations for moving on. 'I wanna see you get your crampons through there.' He watched me delicately stepping a cramponed foot into my one-piece windsuit. With care I guided it into the legging and pulled the unzipped legging back over the boot.

'That's one done successfully. I'll show you.'

'You gonna show me, bud?'

'Yeh, I'm gonna, pal!' Laughter carried out across the great gully.

'Four people on a one-person ledge.'

'Giving a dressing demonstration.'

'With crampons,' added Brett.

'So far so good.'

'These crampons keep coming off. About four times today,' Rajiv complained.

'We'll need to cut slots in the welt of the boot, Rajiv.'

'Rigid crampons would probably be better,' said Brett.

'I asked JP if I could borrow his but he said, "No, I have to climb also."'

'This is what you need,' said Brett, pointing to his crampons. 'Foot fangs. I reckon they're good. A bit heavy, but they're good.'

'I have also used the foot fang. They're very nice. I used them on the Kamet West Ridge. The ice was very hard.'

'The breeze is coming up, isn't it?' Skip remarked, looking out over the névé far below. 'Every day at one-fifteen.' Then turning to me, 'That's a rather complicated harness you've got there, Peter. Like a swami belt with a crotch loop.'

'The best is the Don Whillans sit harness,' pronounced Rajiv.

'Yeh, Don Whillans lives on in every climber's crotch.'

'The sit harness is damn good,' Rajiv's testimonial went on. 'I love it.'

I finished tying my harness in place over my bright red windsuit and the gear clipped on to it jangled in the cool mountain air.

'Well, folks. He's almost ready.'

'Red Riding Hood,' jeered Brett.

'I'll tie into this,' I told them, snapping a figure-eight into the well-anchored placements at the top of the fixed rope.

'I think this is Mamostong.' Rajiv was examining the view. 'Two years ago I was standing on its summit.'

'The round one?'

'Yeh. Not far away really.'

'Somewhere over there is the Shyok Gorge.' We all gazed at the southern skyline with its spectacle of lofty summits.

'What a bunch of cloud piercers!'

'Well,' I paused. 'I can't think of any reason to keep standing here making polite conversation to you lot. So I'll be off and upward. It will probably be best if the belayer perches over there to make optimum use of the rope.'

'There's a good pin in there too.'

'Do you want to belay, Rajiv?'

'Yeh.'

'What are you going to do? Go up on the blue?'

'I think if Rajiv and I go on the blue . . .' I began.

'Although, if you're going to be leading, Rajiv could go up on the blue and he could then belay you up and past him on the red,' reasoned Skip.

'That's a great idea,' I agreed. 'There you are, Rajiv. You climb up to the piton on the blue.'

'Yeh.'

'Tie this one into the anchor.'

'Yeh.'

'Then I'll untie that.'

'Yeh.'

'And I'll climb up on the red.'

'Okay.'

'And you can belay me up to you.'

'Looks like an exciting lead,' remarked Skip.

I led out from the ledge and up a narrow fifty-five-degree finger of ice that rose through the rock and back to the right side of our broad gully. Above me it divided into a handful of chutes and steps that obviously disgorged debris periodically into the central gully. Pinnacles rose above me and I found myself feeling very alone and very vulnerable out there on the front points of my crampons with so much towering overhead and only the rope connecting me with the others out of sight below. I fixed three and a half pitches of rope up the gully before the sun's journey westward cast dark shadows on the South Face and the temperature dropped rapidly, making climbing uncomfortable. Brett, Rajiv and I set up the last belay for the next day's lead before heading back down after Skip. Magan greeted us with hot drinks in the dome tent. Shashank was already seated in the corner cradling a bowl of steaming tea.

'I had too many problems with my crampons,' he explained. 'They came off ten times.'

Looking out of the door of the tent, I stared mesmerised at a strange grey shadow that cut across the otherwise peach-coloured Depsang Plains. It was Rimo's own shadow cast by the setting sun, and just to the south floated the pale orb of the rising moon.

We discussed reducing the size of our group and to my amazement both Rajiv and Magan declared that they were perfectly willing to go down. As they were the two strongest Indian climbers on the expedition I was a little taken aback, especially as Magan had only just reached Camp 1. Later in the night I heard them arguing, followed by Magan's murmuring to his deities and the wafting smell of incense.

A cold and blustery day dawned as we returned to the South Face to continue the climb. Magan and Rajiv ascended the ropes first and fixed three more pitches up to a prominent prow, an isolated rock outcrop just beneath some ice-coated slabs that led to the Rock Band that barred our way to the ridge. Skip and I walked out on to the glacier to view the Rock Band and the upper part of the route, ever on the lookout for a weakness in Rimo's formidable defences. There were no viable alternatives to our current line so we jugged the ropes to where Rajiv was belaying Magan, passing, as we went, both Brett and Shashank who were descending to Advance Base Camp.

Rajiv leaned out over the great slope from his belay, which I hastily rearranged, while he belayed Magan as he moved nervously up the final section of steep ice to the Prow. There was little snow on the bottle-green ice and so he was perched out on his front points and obviously not enjoying the considerable exposure that the lead entailed. Once on the Prow itself he sent a flurry of ice and stones down the face as he chopped a ledge for himself and searched for some protection. I led one more pitch, that evening, out across steep dinner-plate ice that coated the granite slabs above the Prow and beneath the Rock Band. If nothing else, that lead impressed upon me how hard some of the climbing above was going to be. The face rose in a series of unrelenting bulges and buttresses to the shadowed ridge-line and as I peered up at it in the dying light, while I stood on my front points with axe- and hammer-picks driven a mere inch into the hard ice, access to the summit ridge seemed a long way off. I slung a length of rope around a slab that penetrated the ice veneer and abseiled down to the Prow from where we began the long series of abseils down the South Face to the bottom of the mountain.

We were a tired group that huddled into the tent at Seacliff that night to make copious quantities of rehydrating tea and Milo and some simple food.

Skip and I spent the next day exchanging leads slowly above the Prow. It was now cold and overcast and the lack of sun made the steep ice even more brittle. Every time we swung our axes into it, it showered us with shards and large razor-edged plates that skittered off down the face like frisbees. We led three more pitches and cached several ropes up near the top of the day's lead before returning down to the glacier. Back at Seacliff we found Prem, Dave and Terry already ensconced. We gathered in the dome tent to drink hot tea and coffee while Prem joked about our progress on the mountain. 'Tara and I were thinking of taking a stove and a tent and going up the East Face. Maybe we could throw a rope down to you.' Prem laughed alone. 'I hope it would be long enough.' He giggled to himself.

Skip and I prepared to leave for our fourth consecutive day of leading and load-carrying on the South Face. But we had got only a hundred yards from camp when I called out to Skip that I did not have the strength for another hard day and so we plodded rather forlornly back to camp. Magan and Rajiv were also taking a rest day so the mountain was left to Prem, Dave and Terry who planned to carry loads to the top of the fixed ropes and then do some more leading.

Winds gusted over Camp 1 all day – at times reaching fifty to sixty knots – and the tents felt as if they would be uprooted and blown down the glacier like giant tumbleweeds. Skip and I lay in our bags lamenting the lack of mail and talking of home, Elizabeth and Folsom for him, Ann and Woodend for me. Prem, Dave and Terry arrived back late in the evening, exhausted. They had carried their loads as far as the Prow.

At 4.00 a.m. Skip's wristwatch alarm made its high-pitched beep beep and woke him. The purring of the stove right by my ear woke me. We had a bowl of tsampa and departed for the bottom of the fixed ropes at 6.30 a.m. We made good time: forty minutes to the Camel's Back, forty-five minutes to Luncheon Ledge and forty-five up to the Prow where the sun peeped over a spur and glinted off our helmets. I replaced a fixed rope near the Rock Band and Skip led off up the steep white ice just below the Rock Band at 11.00 a.m. For half an hour he struggled to find a belay, during which time Rajiv and Magan caught us up with their packs filled with rope.

'Okay, come on up,' Skip called down to me. 'Belay on.'

It was steep, very exposed and intimidating. 'How are your anchors?' I called up to him.

'There's a reasonable piton,' he attempted to reassure me but didn't because he wasn't.

I continued up the high-angle ice to the shallow outcrop on which Skip had his stance. His reasonable piton was pounded into some rotten granite which further intensified my sense of exposure. I glanced nervously upward. The next lead was mine. We tied off the fixed line below and prepared the climbing rope and the rack of gear I would use on the Rock Band that rose scarily above our heads.

With a ball of tension in my gut I led up an ice-arête above Skip's dubious belay. I looked for a good placement for some protection in the brittle rock but there was nothing of any substance. Above me the ice rose into the Rock Band that jutted out over us. A narrow gut filled with very steep ice led up through the band and into the runnels that we knew lay above and that would almost certainly be active with avalanche debris in certain conditions. Across this lay a slender thread of ice in the back of a groove that I felt would be a feasible route up the Rock Band. But for now I was fifty feet above Skip's marginal belay and without protection in place. I felt very exposed with two thousand feet of steep ice beneath my heels.

'I don't like this,' I called down to Skip. Actually I was scared stiff. I thought of Ann, the farm; how far should I push this? I scrambled upward over seventy degrees of rotten rock to a jug that seemed firm, in a psychological sense, but was not strong. I considered idolising it. It was fissured, crumbling, clearly detached from the substrata and my choice for protection. I had no slings so I tied two nut slings together, looped them over the questionable bollard, snapped the rope into it with some cosmetic relief and called down to Skip.

'Give me tension while I try to climb across to the far side of the gully.' Gingerly I traversed the sixty-degree ice at the bottom of the gully to the foot of the ice-filled groove. It worked. That little fragile bollard had boosted my confidence and had got me across to a clean crack I had spied while scratching for suitable protection. I zealously hammered a Number 5 hexentric into the slot and, as I did so, I could feel my confidence and enthusiasm burgeon. I called down to Skip, 'We're certified safe!' He smiled.

I returned across to the bollard, flicked the makeshift sling free of the tenuous block and returned to the security of the Number 5. Now to climb the groove, I thought as I looked up. The crux was still to come.

The groove was choked with seventy-five-degree ice and the rock that flanked it was near vertical. With grunts and moans as I bridged and jammed, my chest heaving from the exertion at 21,000 feet, I started up the Rock Band. Skip later told me I sounded like a mating hippopotamus, although he acknowledged that it did seem to get results. Thirty feet up the groove I drove the axe in my right hand into the ice while my left hand searched for cracks and crannies in which to find some purchase. Fifty feet above the Number 5 hex was a ledge on to which I struggled and sat there gasping for breath. To my left ran a narrow ledge that led to a gully that would take us to the ridge-line. I looked down at Skip perched on his uncomfortable belay stance. I had climbed the Rock Band.

Edging along the precarious edge on my left I reached the mixed gully where I tied the rope off to a network of nut placements and called down to Skip, Magan and Rajiv to come on up. I was surrounded by excellent piton placements but we had run out of them so I was doubly glad that the ridge was now not too far above us.

Skip led halfway up the face above to the edge of the visible snow patch that we knew led to the ridge. It was getting late,

Skip was finding the lead harder than he had anticipated. Rajiv was shivering.

'We're getting very cold, Skip.' A mumbled response echoed back, most of which was indecipherable and the rest unprintable. A short while later we were on our way down the wall in the extreme cold of evening, checking our equipment carefully before each of the twenty-two rappels that would lower us on to the Camel's Back from where we down-climbed to the glacier and walked wearily back to Seacliff. It had been a long day, twelve hours at the sharp end. Terry met us above the tents and congratulated us on the long-awaited breakthrough.

'Now all we need is to reach the ridge!' We all laughed; a laugh that could almost be a moan. 'Prem went down today,' he went on. 'He's going to organise things down at Advance Base.'

We had barely sat ourselves down in the dome, hardly taken a sip of tea when Rajiv and Magan announced they too were going down.

'To Advance Base?'

'Yes. I cannot go back on to this mountain. I am getting married.' Rajiv explained that he was to be married in exactly one month and he had to stop climbing because his family astrologer had decreed that he should halt all major works one month before the wedding day. In fact, Rajiv told us, he would have to begin his journey back to the plains of India in a few days.

Magan said that he would probably return to Camp 1 to help with the climb. With that they heaved their packs on their backs and walked off into the pale evening light leaving us somewhat lost for words at the abruptness of it all. We decided Prem's descent to Advance Base had influenced Magan's decision. But Rajiv's matrimonial astrology was a complete surprise.

Next day it was Dave and Terry's turn up front. Brett and PV arrived from Advance Base with some supplies and a message at last from Jogindar Singh in New Delhi. Our permit extension would not be a problem. We would be able to have the extra two weeks, taking us to 15 October, before we had to return to Leh. At last some heartening news! But our euphoria was short-lived. No sooner had Brett and PV set off back to Advance Base than Terry and Dave returned from the South Face. As soon as I saw them I knew something must have happened. It was too early in the day for success.

Terry explained. 'We were just below the Prow, mate, and these two massive bloody rock-falls came down. I swear I thought I was a gonna. I leaned in against the rock and prayed. These rocks, the size of your head, flew by. They only just missed us. If I had stuck me hand out they would have hit it.'

'I'm sorry, lads, we're not going to go up when it's raining rocks,' Dave added.

It was a real setback but no one could blame them for turning back. We were glad they were both all right. The warm temperatures and light snow, we reasoned, were probably to blame for the thawing of a piece of critical ice. We would only ascend the face in cold weather from then on, we agreed, although we need not have worried for cold it remained for the rest of our sojourn in the Karakoram.

We were huddled into the dome to brew cups of tea and coffee when Rajiv and Errol arrived from Advance Base with rope and hardware and news from the outside world. Roddy was still sick. Tenzing, the crooked pony contractor, was at Base Camp creating trouble with the pony men, and Jack Morrison had finally arrived there and sent us a letter. It was pretty scathing about the expedition's progress and the level of the water in the Shyok River, and he proceeded to inform us of how precious his time was and how he did not like it to be wasted. I couldn't agree more, I thought. He wanted to leave Base Camp in five days with all the rafts. Prem had read Jack's letter on its way through Advance Base and was clearly incensed by its contents. He had scribbled his own enraged comments on the back.

Skip headed down-valley to see Jack and to try to send a message to Elizabeth; Terry departed to see Prem, and Errol and Rajiv returned to Advance Base. This left a complement of two at Seacliff. Dave and I sat sadly in the dome cooking dinner, and talking forlornly about life and love and the penalties of separation. Dave, of course, had Renée with him on this expedition, but he confessed, 'I feel this trip has been like taking your wife to war.'

The whole expedition seemed to be falling to pieces around us.

Next day was a rest day for Dave and me and just after mid-day we were joined by Brett and Magan once more. Magan told us he had simply wanted to go down to see Prem, and now he was back to climb the mountain. I found his flippancy perplexing. That night I watched him hang a picture of the goddess Durga from the roof of the tent, light incense and recite those timeless incantations that are his religious inheritance.

At 4.00 a.m. Brett started the stove and at 5.00 a.m. four people huddled in the near darkness, their faces lit by the blue tones of the stove's burner and the intermittent yellow beam of a headlamp. I looked across at Brett while he stirred the stewing tea and added more sugar to the pot. He was a quiet man, not without humour, but normally abbreviating his communications to the shortest form. He looked up.

'Do you want some tea?'

'Thanks.'

'Get it yourself,' he said, passing a cup.

By 6.30 a.m. we were on our way across the squeaky dry snow that leads to the Camel's Back where we had cached our harnesses and helmets. I followed Magan up the ropes with a tune sounding in my head that vaguely kept in time with the sliding of the jumars on the rope, my own deep breathing and careful steps up the face. As I ascended I checked the rope for rock-fall damage and scrutinised each anchor as I passed it. At the Prow I caught up with Magan just before the sun peeped over a spur to the east with its warming glow.

'So far so good, Magan. No rock-fall and we've made good time to here.'

'I am going slowly. I am weak,' he said. I was annoyed with his flat response. If there was one thing the whole expedition needed it was a real positive effort.

'You are the strongest Indian climber on the team; surely you can bloody well stop all this complaining?' I broke off then and tried to explain my frustrations. Magan responded appropriately, but for him the mountains are always there and if it is the will of the gods you get up this time, fine, but if not, there will be another time. I simply couldn't feel this philosophical.

We moved on up the ropes across the steep brittle ice of the traverse, up the ice-covered slabs to the sheets of dinner-plate ice beneath the Rock Band. Here we clawed our way up the narrow ice-choked chimney, stemming broadly near the top to obtain purchase, and then sidled along the tiny ledges that led to the mixed pitch where the ropes ended. At 10.50 a.m. I led off up the face above the rock step on steep hard ice. This gave out to loose soft snow on steep granite slabs which made the climbing precarious as my purchase was so unsure. I 'gardened' my way up the face using my ice tools to clear the frozen snow clumps from the upper edges of exposed bulges of rock in order to make available any hand-holds lurking beneath, all the while never knowing whether the hold itself was on something substantial or not. I grovelled and clawed my way up the face and with some relief reached a large belay bollard high on the perimeter of the upper snow-field. That was an exciting moment for above me lay two pitches of medium-grade snow and ice and a final pitch of mixed rock and ice to the ridge. I was delighted and yelled my exuberant information down to Magan who looked up from his narrow belay ledge. I could see Dave on the ice-pitch several hundred feet below as he laboured beneath his pack of food and fuel. Brett was out of sight, probably hidden by the bulk of the Prow.

Magan was soon beside me and offered to take over the lead. He climbed up the snow-field above me for a rope-length and, once I had joined him, continued for another to where the top of the snow-field butted into the final pitch of rock and ice. There he flailed his hammer, called for more rope and scrambled about on his chosen rock outcrop searching for nuances suitable for the none too subtle forms of our remaining hardware.

'Come on up,' he eventually called.

I waved back and began slogging my way up the slope with five ropes, two fuel bottles, a stove, film gear and some personal equipment in my pack. I was beginning to feel the weight of the load on my thighs and calves.

'Look out!'

Whooooof!

Two feet from my ducking head rocketed a block of stone capable of taking my head with it. I looked wildly around, on guard for more artillery, shaken by this close call and feeling pangs of fear run right through me. Then I climbed hurriedly up to Magan, inspected the state of his marginal anchor and set off up a steep ice-gully hemmed in by two shattered ribs that rose to the skyline. I hammered a blade into a good crack a short way up and felt much better for it; at least my presence on this face was now secured. I climbed on, resting occasionally by clipping into my ice-axe with its pick driven into the hard ice above my head. Fifty feet up I climbed left on to the rock and popped a Number 2 friend into a verglassed groove, tugged on it to check it, snapped the rope into it and climbed on.

A small hollow filled with snow led through a band of rock above and this led into a gently inclined bowl of soft snow.

At the head of this the dazzling white snow met the intense blue of the sky. It was the top of the South Face and the long-striven-for ridge-line. I was saturated with emotion. We had fought for this for so long. I felt the battle had been waged since we left Australia and now we were getting somewhere.

The rope came tight so I put my axe into the snow and tied the rope to it. Taking off my pack I retrieved another rope which I tied to the lead rope and continued plugging up to the ridge. Just down from the crest was a suitable site and there I pounded a deadman anchor into the snow and with a clove hitch secured our fixed line to the ridge-top.

'Come on up, Magan. I'm on the ridge!'

All about me lay the barren mountains of the Depsang and China spread north and east, the white bulky giants of Mamostong and Saser Kangri dominated our southern horizon and west, through the parabolic walls of the Ibex Col, lay a breathtaking throng of granitic spires and block-topped peaks that crowd the Siachen Glacier area. Directly above me rose the South-East Ridge of Rimo and to the right I could see Rimo's summit. A fluted face led to this tiny untrod pedestal; it seemed so close, so eminently accessible. To the north was Rimo II, a mere shoulder on the massif, and Rimo III and IV rose dominantly across the northern horizon.

I turned and gazed down the heavily glaciated eastern flank of Rimo. Huge crevasses and ice-cliffs, blocks of avalanche debris and far below upon the vast-textured, moraine-striped expanse of ice, the South Rimo Glacier, I could just make out the dome tent at Advance Base: a golden-yellow bubble like a grain of sand upon the ice. It was about five miles away horizontally and nearly four thousand feet below where I stood. I wondered if anyone there could see me. Or even expected me to be where I was.

Again and again I gazed around me. The vista was intoxicating! Karakoram, Yarkand, Tienshan, Depsang, Siachen, Shyok, Nubra, Ladakh and Baltoro.

The rope flexed and Magan's bearded face appeared from the wall below. His gap-toothed grin showed his pleasure of the moment and we happily shook each other's hands and pounded one another's backs.

'We've done it, Magan. We really are going to get up this mountain now. It looks so close from here.' I felt those days of doubt slip behind me and was filled with a second wind of summit enthusiasm.

'It is your determination that has done it,' he responded. 'I did not think we would get this far with the weather and all that.' There was a silence; one of awe and elation. 'At last. This is a great day.'

Over the next two hours we dug a tent platform, pitched the tent for Camp 2, helped Dave and Brett up on to the ridge and rejoiced in the sheer magnificence of the Karakoram. And all the while the sun shone and there was not a breath of wind on the ridge.

When the sun dipped behind Rimo's southern shoulder we departed, rappelling down rope after rope; I left my helmet and harness at the Camel's Back and, picking up my ski pole, walked back to Seacliff. Skip had arrived and was brewing tea for us as we arrived. He had come all the way from Base Camp and his news of the camps down the glacier was a convoluted tale of micro-political intrigues. I wanted to remain in my mountain euphoria and leave all those problems alone.

10

So Close and Yet So Far
25 September – 5 October

A rest day followed where the only things exercised were our voice boxes. Terry arrived from Advance Base with the latest stories from down the glacier. Roddy had amoebic dysentery and had not eaten for four days. JP intended to return up the glacier to climb on the mountain. Jack planned to raft down the Shyok with two of the rafts pending approval by the army GOC, and Shashank, Miriam and several others intended to go with him. Prem had sent a message to army HQ requesting a twenty-four-hour reply, asking whether PV could accompany the rafting group and Prem become the new official liaison officer for the expedition party. No reply was ever received.

That afternoon the weather began to deteriorate with banks of frontal cloud sweeping in from the south-east. Terry's battered radio delivered news of widespread flooding on the plains of India and that the Indo-Australian cricket match had been washed out. We were all disappointed with that news as we had taken a round of bets on the final score. So we tuned in to Radio Australia, a bizarre experience for a tent full of expeditionaries in Central Asia to be listening to Aussie accents and Australian rules football. We took bets on the results of the game in Melbourne; it was won by the Hawks and Dave had the closest score.

It was snowing when we rose at 4.00 a.m. next morning

and the weather appeared to be here to stay. We spent the morning reading and writing and, later, I talked with Magan and asked him what his family felt about his climbing expeditions.

'Previously when I went to the mountains for courses and expeditions,' Magan began, 'they did not know about climbing and the mountaineering. None of my family nor my community nor my town went in for such intensive climbing. So I used to tell them that I was going for the tourism trip, for some teaching and all. So they thought that he has just gone to enjoy the mountains. Like Simla and Manali.'

'Like going to a resort town?'

'Yes. One time I took my mother to the Garhwal. You know the Garhwal is a holy place to the Hindus and my mother is quite orthodox. I took her to the Gormuk, where the Ganges begins, and she felt very greatly when she saw the mountains, all snow covered and very sharp. That was when she began to worry about my trips. I was not just visiting the hill stations. But by then I had some kind of a name in India. So my parents were feeling proud and did not try to stop me. But they were always worried. Like on the Everest Expedition, there was news every day in the newspapers and the radio and in 1985, when I fell on the summit ridge, they didn't sleep all night. You know I am from a traditional family and they became so worried that my mother, my brother and three, four other relatives came all the way to the Kathmandu to see me. They did not want me to go on the expedition. It is not like Western countries where there are different attitudes. Your family and your wife allow you to go. There is no problem.'

'It's not that easy,' I argued.

'For us the Himalaya is holy. When I go I worship the area, I worship the mountain as a god. Every stone that I climb I regard highly to keep me safe. People ask why the Himalaya is a god. It is because the Himalaya gives life to the Indian plains – water, weather, everything. I am also from an orthodox family. I worship goddess Durga, my family too. So I feel every time proud that I am in a holy area, especially in the Garhwal Himalaya. If there is any heaven it is in the Himalaya, it is in the mountains.'

About 1.00 p.m. Errol and Dorje arrived at Seacliff with more food and the latest news update from other camps. The Shyok was a mere trickle of its former self because the extremely low temperatures slowed down the melt. Jack and company had abandoned their intention to raft the river and planned to return to Leh or remain at Base Camp until we finished the climb. Errol and Dorje returned down to Advance Base with the good news about our having established Camp 2 on the ridge and we all returned to the serious business of reclining in our sleeping bags and waiting for the weather to improve. All up, the day was of a taciturn nature and averaged out at inclement.

Another day and again the weather was bad. Magan and Skip descended to Advance Base Camp to get some urgently needed food and fuel and to discuss our tactics with Prem. When they returned they told us that Advance Base was also nearly out of food and that Prem and Tara had decided to return to Leh and eventually Manali; they had left Advance Base that morning to descend to Base Camp. Prem had assured Magan and Skip that he would send further supplies up the glacier and that Shashank and Wangchuk would take over Advance Base. The expedition's state of flux was continuing, I thought. The weather was atrocious and time was running out on our permit. I sat in the dome with Terry and Brett, listening to the snow on the roof.

Prem's latest decision to leave the expedition had come as another shock after he had so successfully invigorated it not long before. But he was not involved in the actual climbing and, as food and time were running out, presumably he decided that the small group of climbers at Camp 1 was all that was actively involved with the expedition's objectives, so all others might just as well depart. Whatever his reasons were, he never told any of us. Only Tara knew what Prem thought of our state of affairs and he was not about to pass this information on to anyone.

As we did religiously every night, we tuned into the All India radio broadcast from New Delhi to hear the weather forecast for mountaineering expeditions. Through the whistling and whirring and crackling of the reception came the familiar voice with its slow, clear pronunciation, a voice that seemed to mouth each and every syllable for the sheer joy of it.

'This is All India Radio broadcasting on . . .' strange inter-galactic sounds interrupted '. . . kilohertz. Here is the special weather bulletin for the Dobin Expedition.' A shrill whistling sound cut across the transmission causing us all to lean towards the radio, straining our ears. Dobin was us, a code-name given us for radio transmissions because we were in a high security area. 'For the next twenty-four hours commencing from 1200 hours Greenwich Mean Time there will be a generally cloudy sky with a few showers. Light snowfall likely above 13,000 feet. Wind and temperature for 3.1 kilo-metres above sea level: thirty kilometres per hour, eight degrees Celsius. At 4.5 kilometres above sea level: thirty kilometres per hour, minus two degrees Celsius. At 5.8 kilometres above sea level: thirty kilometres per hour, tem-perature minus eighteen degrees Celsius. At 7.6 kilometres above sea level: thirty kilometres per hour, temperature minus nineteen degrees Celsius. At 9.5 kilometres above sea level: a very strong westerly, sixty kilometres per hour, temperature minus thirty-eight degrees Celsius. Outlook for the next twenty-four hours: improvement is rather likely, winds likely to strengthen. And that is the end of the special weather forecast for the Dobin Expedition.'

'Typical,' sighed Terry as the wind roared outside the tent, making the walls pulse as if they were alive.

'Happy birthday, Skip!'

It was his thirty-ninth. The date was 28 September and we

had hoped to be on top of Rimo to celebrate but that was not to be. The snow fell more heavily than ever that day and about a foot of the stuff gathered round our tents. There was no alternative to sitting in the dome and consuming what delicacies we had accumulated for the birthday party: Ladakhi bread (not dissimilar to bricks), chocolate drinks, yesterday's rice pilau with a can of mushrooms stirred into it, biscuits of the excessively dry variety, canned cheese, tomato soup accompanied by some rash betting on the outcome of the Indo-Pakistani hockey match at the Asian Games in Seoul. It amused us at the time that both countries were threatening to boycott the games because the maps exhibited in Korea misrepresented their claimed borders. The disputed ground lay right beneath the floor of the yellow dome.

Next day we discussed the situation and came to the only solution open to us: descent. The weather continued to be terrible and we had nearly exhausted the food and fuel at Camp 1.

At Base Camp we found that Roddy was well again after his severe bout of amoebic dysentery and keen to return to the mountain. But Shashank had already departed for Leh, with bridegroom Rajiv and Jack and all the rafts. Prem and Tara had changed their plans again and said they would stay on to the end of the expedition.

I was sitting outside my tent pondering our predicament when I saw four ponies and some men following the track down the moraines and on to the glacier ice. At first I took them for the sharp end of our caravan come to start taking our equipment out to Sasoma. But they were soldiers and they had been sent to watch over us. They pitched their tents below our camp, set up their radio beside PV's aerial on the moraines above camp and maintained their distance.

Prem was concerned by the arrival of the soldiers and suspected that something had happened, or would soon. 'Jack should have been escorted by PV from this area. It could cause some trouble. This is a very sensitive border area,' he told Skip.

Eventually he called an expedition meeting. Prem sat on a boulder near the kitchen tent and we gathered around in a circle. He was the distinguished Colonel, we were his men. He recapped on some of the recent developments before turning to the future.

'There is time for one more attempt on the mountain but not very much time. We must leave Base Camp on the sixth and, if necessary, the mountaineering team could leave one or two days later and catch up with the pony caravan. I will work with the support team and ensure that the necessary supplies are carried up the glacier. We will begin to dismantle the camps and bring equipment that is not needed down to Base Camp. I think the attempt on the peak should be made by Skip, Magan, Peter and whoever else is strong at the time, probably Terry, Brett or Dave. As soon as there is an improvement in the weather we must start. Any questions?'

There was a silence broken only by the 'craw, craw' of a spectator crow on the moraine wall that overlooked the proceedings.

'Wangchuk.'

'Sir.'

'When can we get the ponies here?'

'Five days, sir.'

'How many will we need?'

'I think twenty-five would be sufficient, sir. We can bring them here and keep them until we are ready to go.'

I looked about me and at the few mangy ponies that Stopdan had recently brought up. What would they live on? Once they reached the fodderless environs of Base Camp their time here would be limited. I had already observed these horses sorting through their own faeces for undigested grain and fibre. The extreme cold was another good reason for keeping up the momentum.

'You organise the ponies and prepare for the evacuation

of the camp. The climbers should prepare for the last attempt. Do you agree?'

There were muffled affirmatives in several languages. Prem rose from his granite seat and returned to his tent. We were dismissed.

Prem certainly had better connections than the rest of us. Within hours of the meeting the great curtain of cloud was drawn back and Rimo was again exposed at the head of the South Rimo Glacier. We were able to see our Camp 2 site and this was encouraging: not only was it high, but it appeared high on the South-East Ridge as well and a good distance towards the summit.

'Just where a Camp 2 should be,' declared Dave.

JP, Wangchuk and Stopdan were to leave the next morning with Stopdan's two ponies. JP would organise our affairs in Leh and Delhi ahead of the main caravan, while Wangchuk and Stopdan would recruit the additional ponies we needed to evacuate. We had heard that Tenzing Dorje, our *bête noire*, was still at Saser Brangsa with, it was rumoured, many ponies. So obtaining horses could either prove straight-forward or a manipulated business transaction by a man who knew we had no alternatives. Both Brett and Terry begged to differ here as they yearned to administer a knuckle sand-wich to this man in the belief that it would work wonders.

That evening the Dobin Expedition weather forecast dem-onstrated its perennial lack of commitment to anything radical, like clear skies and fine weather or even a terrible storm that would uproot our tents and blow us all away, by announcing in its sobering way that 'little change is expected'.

We returned to our tents to pack away unnecessary gear and to scribble last-minute notes to the outside world. Judg-ing by our mail delivery situation to date I felt the likeliest way for these communications to reach their destinations would be to chuck a message in a bottle into the Shyok River.

*

Rimo stood out stark and magnificent as we left camp on 1 October. Next morning Brett, Dave and Roddy pushed on from Camp 1 to Luncheon Ledge, pulling frozen ropes out of the deep snow as they climbed. Terry, Skip, Magan and I waited in the dome, sorting equipment to take up to Camp 2 the next day.

'Magan, what are your thoughts for tomorrow?'

'I am over-optimistic. We will have a nice warm day, good fitness, good route so, now, no problem.'

'Terry, would you describe your original involvement in this expedition as masochistic or foolhardy?'

'I would describe it as easily those and possibly more. Indeed, I'd go so far as to say this is probably one of the best areas for masochists. We could even sell it as "the masochists' trek" to one of the trekking companies.'

'Do you think you have aged on this expedition, Skip?' I asked.

'Fifty, perhaps sixty years.'

It was still dark as we left Seacliff on 3 October in the thirty-below-zero-temperatures, clouds of white condensation blasting from our mouths as we plugged steps in the deep snow up the glacier to the Camel's Back. We geared up and began the long and arduous ascent, tearing the rope out of the frozen snow above us as we inched higher on the face beneath our loads. At Luncheon Ledge we loaded more equipment into our packs and climbed on up the great gully, often having to dig the rope out of the snow with our ice-axes. At the Prow I felt waves of nausea run through me, a legacy of our visit to Base Camp and Jonga's kitchen, and slumped on the ropes while Skip maintained the lead on to the ice-coated slabs. An hour later I resumed the lead from Skip and continued on up the steep ice to the Rock Band where I wriggled awkwardly beneath my load as I climbed the rock groove and sidled along the narrow ledges to the snow-covered slabs. Before each rope-length I pulled heavily on the rope to check that it didn't have any terminal damage and to wrench it free from the snow. Looking down I could see Roddy moving up steadily after us, although Terry was falling further and further behind. As I set off into the final gully I had seen Roddy set off from the Prow far below and Terry, sadly, beginning to descend. He was sick as a dog, Roddy told me later, and really depressed about having to go down.

By mid-afternoon we reached the solitary tent on the ridge, our Camp 2 site. Magan, Skip and I pitched a second tent and began producing hot drinks on the kerosene stove. Roddy arrived just as the sun slipped behind the South-East Shoulder and we all crawled into the tiny tents to feed ourselves and sleep.

I slept well, apart from the multiple exits necessitated by copious cups of tea earlier in the night. Outside the stars were bright and clear and as the sun rose a cold pale blue light spread over the Depsang.

After several large bowls of sweet tea Magan and Roddy set off up the elegant snow-ridge above the camp on what was supposed to be a brief trail-blazing reconnaissance. The snow on the ridge was far deeper than we had anticipated and their progress reflected the conditions. Pitch after laboured pitch they plugged a trench towards a platform from where the ridge continued at a less steep angle. Near this point Magan called out and looking up I saw the slope break away, sending a slough down the South Face, cascading over the rock bluffs down towards the Ibex Col Glacier. They continued only a short distance beyond this point, far enough to see that there were another dozen pitches to the final summit ridge silhouetted above us against the azure skies.

On return to the camp they were both tired and demoralised. 'The snow's horrendously deep and it's all unstable. Did you see the avo' that Magan set off?' Roddy was feeling despondent about the route and pessimistic about our chances. 'I'm going to sleep for the rest of the day,' he declared as he gulped down some soup that Skip had handed him. He looked around him. The elixir seemed to have helped. 'But it's the most beautiful view I've ever seen.'

The vista was magnificent. Our spectacular pedestal afforded views of steep granite peaks, broad névés, rubble-strewn plateaux and aerial panoramas of several nations.

Magan had maintained a somewhat stoic reticence since his return to camp. Now he cleared his voice and spoke. 'I will not continue tomorrow. I will be going down.'

We had heard all this before, of course. But after all we had striven for and achieved, we just couldn't believe he was going to toss it in now.

'I will carry some gear for you tomorrow up to where Roddy and I got to. Then I will go down,' he concluded.

I put down my soup. 'Never in my life have I struck so many people giving up on a single expedition. Everyone seems to want to go home. Did they think that Rimo was going to be one glorious walk? Surely we should give it one last try? We're so close! A couple of days and we could be on the summit. If we can't climb it then, so be it. But let's try.'

I retreated to my tent feeling wretched.

Skip leaned in the door and grinned at me. 'I'm not giving up,' he said.

The afternoon drifted by with jottings in our journals, talk of other adventures, plans for the next day and thoughts of far away.

Pale sunset colours washed over the peaks and glaciers, turning the great glacial sheets of ice to shimmering bronze. As the sun dipped behind Rimo the temperature plummetted, forcing us reluctantly into our tents and the warmth of our sleeping bags. Soon the two stoves were chugging towards cooking a co-operative dinner. Main course from Skip and my tent, drinks and water-bottle refills from Magan and Roddy's.

I enjoyed the chores involved in cooking and tending the

stove. Perhaps it was therapeutic. Scooping snow into the pot to create some water in which to cook noodles and a meat-and-tomato sauce; all the while attending the stove as it hissed and spluttered when drops of water spilled on to the burner. Periodically I peered out of the open tent door to the fading lights in the sky beyond, with the cocoon of Roddy and Magan's tent in the foreground and through the nylon their darting headlamps as they tended their own stove.

'Pass your bowls, you guys,' I called. Roddy's head appeared from the opposite tent and tossed two plastic bowls across the snow platform to me. I ladled steaming hot food into these and shunted them back across the slick snow to Roddy's outstretched hands. Then the process was reversed as we had our hot chocolate and refilled our water bottles which we stored inside our sleeping bags to prevent them from freezing during the night. By six o'clock all was quiet at Camp 2. Only stars remained out; only they could sustain the extreme cold.

Skip made yet another exit from our sardine-can tent, then gruffly began starting the stove. Apparently some inanimate objects were vindictively sliding into his way so he tossed them all aside with a clatter and continued with the fingertip-freezing business of starting our obstinate stove. It was 5.00 a.m. The eastern sky promised light and warmth but that would not be for another hour so the stove antics would have to proceed without the encouragement of the sun.

Since I had cooked the dinner I considered it Skip's turn to cook the breakfast, although my unilateral view was not, quite obviously, being reciprocated. Again and again the stove ran low, requiring attention, as we both, stubbornly, lay deep inside our bags waiting for the other to remedy the situation. At 6.25 a.m. the sun's light and glorious life-giving heat struck the tent and coincided with the pot reaching the boil. I felt rejuvenated. Our little duel was forgotten.

'What are you making?' I called to Roddy and Magan. 'Why don't you make the drinks and Skip can make the porridge?'

'Ha, ha,' Skip grumbled from within his sleeping bag.

'Okay,' came a muffled voice from the other tent.

In the bitter cold we finished our breakfast and packed away the sleeping bags, the tents, stoves and climbing equipment. By the time we began to ascend the ropes Roddy and Magan had left in position the sun was climbing higher into the sky and sapped our strength. We laboured beneath our packs up the ridge to the platform where Magan and Roddy had halted the day before. Here Magan carried out his decision to descend. 'Good luck,' he said solemnly and without further ado turned and descended the ropes to the two tent platforms which was all that was left of Camp 2.

Once Magan had finished with the ropes we pulled them up, loading the extra gear on to our packs, and continued on up the crest of the ridge. The further we climbed the more exposed it became; to the south the ridge dropped away down the South Face and on the north side it was just as precipitous as it fell away over a convex ice bulge that teetered 500 feet above the hanging glacier on the eastern side of the mountain. We reached a small level section and here we left our packs. Skip and Roddy returned down a short distance to retrieve some gear and I soloed on up the ridge to plug some steps unladen and to check the route.

I hadn't gone far. Perhaps a hundred yards. The snow was between one and two feet deep and I had noted some distinct layering, characteristic of wind slab. I continued as the snow was becoming firmer and less deep as I climbed on to a more exposed knoll in the ridge-line. This led into a steeply rising crest that rose to a complex section of unstable-looking cornices. Here the snow became deeper again.

CRACK!

The slope beneath me suddenly broke free and poured off down the southern side, plunging over the bluff immediately below me. I froze and looked carefully around in order to survey my escape potential. There wasn't much, nor would you expect there to be on a knife-edge ridge. Above, the ridge got steeper and to go on I would need to have a rope. After what had just happened I felt I needed a rope to descend as well. Both Roddy and Skip were out of sight so I decided to reverse down to the platform immediately. I had taken two steps when – BOOM! – the entire slope settled, further demonstrating its structural instability. I turned, faced out from the slope and almost ran down the narrow ridge to the spot where we had left our packs.

After a council of war Roddy roped up and Skip belayed him from just below the knoll as he struck off up the unstable ridge to the top of my tracks and then forged a short way further on. Often he sank into the snow up to his thighs and the effort involved made him pant and lean face-in against the slope. I pulled out the little Super 8 movie camera and filmed his progress.

'Aah!' Roddy had taken another step and as he began to transfer his weight upward the slope collapsed. He had disappeared. I kept the camera rolling and searched the viewfinder.

Roddy's hand and axe swung out of the hole he had dropped into and with difficulty he scrambled out of the peculiar ridge-top crevasse whose rim kept disintegrating further back on both sides, exposing a six-foot-wide hole.

Roddy struggled to regain his breath and shouted down to us. 'What's a crevasse doing on a ridge? It goes down a long way. The whole ridge is in pretty bad condition.'

'How does it look above where you are? It seems to level out a short way on.'

'I'll have a look.' He reached above his head and swung his axe into the snow above the crevasse, chopping repeatedly to clear the loose snow. Then he drove the pick into the rim and pulled energetically up on it. Kicking his crampons into the far side of the slot he hauled himself up and over the crevasse. Continuing, he kicked his crampons into the crest and worked his way slowly to where it narrowed further and the angle reduced. A cornice extended out over the northern side of the ridge so Roddy dropped on to the south side and climbed along just below the corniced crest. It was so narrow here that at one point his ice-axe pierced the ridge and protruded on the north side.

'Fifteen feet!' roared Skip.

'That's all the rope?' Roddy barked back.

'That's it.'

'I'll have to down-climb. There's nowhere solid to belay here.' Roddy retraced his moves along the slender edge of the precarious ridge to a tiny pedestal fifty feet above the crevasse. He stood there and looked down at Skip and me and shook his head. 'The snow's in really bad shape. I think if we go on we'll be taking some big risks.' He paused. 'I'm going to come down.'

'Okay. Skip, will you belay me so that I can go up and have a look?'

'Sure,' he responded.

As soon as Roddy was down I tied into the climbing rope and ascended the ridge to the crevasse and then continued up to the pedestal. Ahead of me lay a paper-thin ridge, tilted in waves from side to side; ridge-line origami. And even on terrain as wild as this the snow was insubstantial; 'sugary rubbish' Roddy had called it. I had to agree. I put in a reasonable belay on the pedestal and called down to Skip to come on up.

He had already made up his mind, I think. Nevertheless he began up the ridge towards me, stopping at the lip of the crevasse. He struggled there for a while and then looked up at me. 'What do you think of it up there?'

'Not much. It's hard to say whether we can climb along the ridge with it in this condition or not.'

'Not the ridge; the weather.'

My concentration on the climb had enabled me to ignore

the meteorological developments that were sweeping in from the north-east. Already we were engulfed in cloud and the wind was rising. It was not supposed to today. I agreed to descend so we could talk about it. Should we wait until the next day and hope the snow would have improved? It was snowing by now so that seemed unlikely.

'Frankly,' I said, 'I think it's too dangerous as it is. We're so bloody close and yet so far.'

No one wanted to pronounce the final decision and no one individual did. We all simply began to descend. We had reached about 22,500 feet and the summit lay another 800 feet above us. We rappelled several pitches and down-climbed the rest to Camp 2. It was evening and in another couple of hours it would be dark. I decided to descend immediately. I packed a heavy pack and set off down the fixed ropes below the camp for the last time. Skip and Roddy remained at Camp 2 for the night and descended the next day, stripping the route as they went.

Suddenly our adventure had come to an end. Or so we thought.

PART THREE

DESCENT

11

A Difficult Journey
6 – 30 October

We found Advance Base an abandoned mess. Most of the gear had not been carried down and it was like somewhere after an air strike. This heightened our anxieties about what was developing down at Base Camp. I think we all felt there were bad vibrations afoot. Dave went ahead to find out what was going on down-valley and the rest of us set to the task of dismantling Seacliff before attempting to sort out the chaos of Advance Base. We couldn't carry all the equipment so we agreed that we would have to ferry it to the dump and then down to Base Camp from there. With forty kilos on our backs we trudged, back-sore and brain-numb, down the medial moraine to the dump where Skip found a note left an hour or two before by Dave who had come up the glacier from Base Camp to help with ferrying gear down.

> Dear Team,
>   It was extremely important that you all came down today. There are only nine horses at Base Camp and all horses leave together tomorrow.

He went on to say how Jack had been arrested with Rajiv, and Shashank, and that they were being marched at gun-point over the Saser La by some soldiers. He suggested that all our film could be confiscated by the army. Prem and Tara had left Base Camp the previous day to attempt to defuse the situation and Magan, Wangchuk and the cookboy had refused to return up the glacier to help with the evacuation.

Base Camp has run out of food. Honestly, there is only dhal, black tea and chappattis.
Suffice to say that I cannot hold the horses and none can be left behind, so Base Camp will evacuate tomorrow.
Hope to see you soon.

Dave.

This was devastating news. We hastily made some plans. Skip and I would lighten our loads a little and race down the glacier to try and hold the caravan, while Terry, Brett and Roddy would camp at the dump and ferry the rest of the gear down from Advance Base early the next morning. Skip and I departed into the spreading gloom of both the evening and our prospects.

It was pitch black as we followed the yellow beams of our headlamps into Base Camp to meet Dave and Magan.

'What's the plan for tomorrow, Magan? You know the others are out of food up there and are ferrying down the rest of the gear tomorrow. A lot of that equipment belongs to the IMF.'

Magan, short-fused Magan, was primed and ready. He went off with an irrational rush. 'I don't care about the equipments. We have the order from Colonel to leave tomorrow at 9.00 a.m. and so we must carry out this order. Colonel has made me the leader. I will make the decision.'

Our climbing partner had transformed himself into a petty high-altitude bureaucrat who knew he had the upper hand and as our new leader his new-found authority had gone to his head.

'Magan, did you hear what I said? The others have no food, they are carrying your gear down the glacier. All we have to do is to wait one day and we can all leave together. The expedition complete.'

'I don't need to listen to you,' he scowled. 'It is the order.

We will leave tomorrow. I don't care about the equipments or about the others. They should have come down today.' With that he retreated into his sleeping bag, pulling it up over his face so that we could not see him.

The next day Skip and I rose early, packed some of the expedition gear, a little of which would go out on the ponies, and after farewelling the caravan, Skip, Dave and I returned up the glacier to the dump. My ill humour carried me over those icy miles in one hour and fifty minutes, just in time for tea with Roddy, Terry and Brett who had recently returned from Advance Base with the rest of the gear. I found it hard to tell them the truth although I knew they already suspected the facts.

Again it was dark when we arrived back at the deserted Base Camp site where not a tent was standing. It was thirty below zero. Before turning in I went for a lonely and depressing stroll, and for the first time saw a sign of native fauna. A small mouse-like creature without a tail scurried on its way across the boulders as it no doubt surveyed the plentiful winter supplies that were scattered around. Looking up the glacier, Rimo stood in a swirl of cloud and I could hear the dull hum of a storm on the peak.

So, having evacuated the camps on the mountain and Advance Base without any help, we began the distasteful job of clearing up the mess left behind by the others and particularly Jonga. We made up our packs to 45 kilos each and the 250 kilos of equipment that was left was inventoried and stowed for a caravan we hoped would arrive to uplift it in the near future. There was almost no food or fuel left so the long trek out was going to be a hungry one.

When the time came to depart from Base Camp we had a militaristic lowering of the flag and a ceremonial incineration of the sponsor's banner and at 1.30 p.m. we left camp beneath our huge loads. The walk was delightful along the vegetated side of the sérac-ed glacier with a sense of freedom being enhanced by the appearance of hares and those creatures we had sagely decided were LBBs, little brown birds. Reluctantly we dropped down on to the Shyok River flats and moved off across the infinity of its expanse. By now we were struggling beneath our colossal packs.

By about 5.30 p.m. Rimo had receded into the background, as had the great snouts of both the South Rimo and Central Rimo Glaciers. We were not going to reach Gepshan as planned to rendezvous with PV, who had insisted that he remain behind there in order to accompany us further. As all light diminished to a fuzzy grey we stopped by a braid of the river and pitched our camp.

From the boulders and gravel of the river flats we climbed on to the gentle meadow of Gepshan, an area of luxuriant mosses and clear-water brooks that tumbled and bubbled their meandering ways among the clumps of moss and pale green grasses. A veritable asylum from the harshness of an imminent Karakoram winter. It was refreshing to be able to enjoy the scents and softness underfoot of alpine vegetation. Skip and I revelled in it as we marched purposefully down-valley.

'Over there, Skip.' I pointed to a round outcrop on the river side of the meadow. 'They're keeping an eye on us. There will probably be soldiers stationed all over the place.' The silhouette of a figure stood motionless on the hillock, testimony to Prem's concerns that the army had become interested in our presence.

He appeared before us like a phantom sitting tall on his pony and facing us. I had not seen where he came from and, despite spotting the scout earlier, his sudden emergence startled me. He began to dismount as we approached and from what I could see he was unarmed. In a smattering of broken English, and pointing back towards the military camp three miles away across the immense river flats, he conveyed his message. 'Wait here. Captain sahib coming.' He sustained a stoical locked-jaw visage, the way one does when awaiting the drill at the dentist. He looked out on to the great river flats and following his line of vision I managed to locate some minuscule antlike objects upon the grey of the river plain. One was on horseback and the others on foot.

'It's the Gepshan welcoming committee.'

'They've got nothing to do out here. We're the biggest news since the 'sixty-two war and they all want to take advantage of it.'

The swarm of tiny ants had transformed into men and they were now only a few hundred yards away. The foot soldiers were armed. They could have been part of Genghis Khan's ferocious armies for, it occurred to me, nothing had really altered in these parts over the millennia. Only the epaulettes had changed.

'Here comes the officer.'

A horseman ascended into view from the banks and deep gullies at the brink of the meadow. He was a slight man wearing an over-sized Cossack hat made from a black fur. A pair of tinted glasses were perched upon the slender bridge of his nose and a smile lay creased across his face. I wasn't sure whether this was a good sign or an ominous one.

He dismounted before us, handing the reins to the soldier with the locked-jaw problem. He extended his hand towards Terry who had stepped forward.

'Hello. How are you?' Terry asked apprehensively.

'I am very fine.'

'I am Terry Ryan.' They shook hands.

'I am Captain Sinna.' His voice died away towards the end of his name as if he wished he had not disclosed it.

'Do you have any horses that we could use?'

'No, I cannot give you any.'

'Our packs weigh over forty kilos and they are really crippling us.'

'No, they cannot be that heavy,' responded Captain Sinna, who was obviously the sort of man who had never carried anything in his life heavier than his handtowel when he was about to have a wash. He gestured to the mountain of packs and instructed his subordinate to test the weight of one. The soldier grasped mine, a hand on either side, and, with the skis waving about as he strained to lift it, pronounced it to be twelve kilos, maybe.

'Bloody bullshit,' mumbled Brett.

'These men,' the captain pointed at his soldier, 'are used to carrying big loads. These are nothing to them.'

'Who is he? Superman?'

A group of foot soldiers scrambled up the banks of the river-bed and gathered around us. They were a sour-faced bunch.

'Do you want some tea?' asked Captain Sinna.

'That would be very nice,' answered Terry.

'Do you have a pot and some tea-leaves?' continued the captain.

We were all thirsty and so the tea-break was a welcome one. PV arrived at this time with a cheesy grin on his face.

'We came looking for you yesterday. You were not coming. So again today we have come.'

'Thank you for the tea, Captain.'

'It is my pleasure.'

We were beginning to feel that all was well with the army and that they would allow us to proceed.

'I have something to say,' spoke up the captain, his voice reaching a higher pitch. We listened with growing apprehension.

'I am going to search your baggages. You will line up in front of me. In a straight line. Take everything out of your bags.'

'You mean unload everything from our packs?'

'Do it now,' he yelled. 'I am going to take all of your exposed film. Do not hide any film from me. It will be destroyed.'

We began this task, mumbling reflections of our annoyance as we did so.

'Move along,' snapped Skip as he began laying out the contents of his carefully packed load.

'Why don't you?'

'Line up!' screamed the diminutive captain. 'You will do as I tell you. There will be no discussion. You will line up in a row; a straight line. If you do not do as I say then I will not treat you as gentlemen,' he shrieked. I felt he was enjoying himself and, looking round, I noted that the soldiers had their guns at the ready. One order – just one order – and we were history.

'Now do as I say! Do it now!'

One by one they searched the contents of our packs, even feeling through the down of our sleeping bags for hidden films. They thoroughly frisked us and all this under the watchful eye of Captain Sinna and his armed foot soldiers. Every roll of exposed film was taken and deposited in a large bag which a soldier tied into a swag.

We were a sullen group. It was as if it had been a part of ourselves that had been taken. The film represented more than just celluloid to us. It was an expression of self and it carried the weight of being a critical component of the expedition's sponsorship, too.

'Don't touch me,' Skip remonstrated with old Lockjaw.

'We are going to check your person,' Captain Sinna asserted. 'Do not resist.'

'Are you a married man, Major?' inquired Dave, subtly promoting Captain Sinna a rank, something that he quite obviously appreciated. Dave drew him into a banal conversation centred on himself, a topic for which he showed an unabashed preference.

'I am coming from the same place in New Delhi as Errol. We are the neighbours.'

'That's fantastic. What a small world.'

'The world is small but India is still big,' said PV with a giggle as he came up behind us.

We walked away from the scene of our detention feeling

demoralised. Our pace slowed, Brett was having trouble with his right knee and by mid-afternoon had become quite disabled.

'Now you do not have as much to carry,' joked the lightly laden PV. 'The army has taken your film so the loads are not so heavy.'

Only one hour separated the site of the army's violation of ourselves and our possessions and where we stopped to camp. Here the river drove its full force into an overhung bluff at the entrance of the gorge and a strong cold draught accelerated up the narrow venturi in the valley below.

That evening we cooked the meagre remains of what food we had. A diluted tomato soup poured over a handful of instant noodles and washed down by black tea with a hint of sugar was our lot and the source of the next day's energy. We were all looking haggard and even the well-muscled specimens among us, Roddy and Skip, were becoming like the rest – stick insects. A depression of spirit and the cloud of exhaustion led us into an uncomfortable sleep.

With the morning we slung our over-laden packs on to our backs and set off down the river flat. It had been an exceptionally cold night and the evidence of this lay on the banks of the river. Ice reached two yards out into the swiftly flowing water and, to our astonishment, we could see that a sludge of large ice crystals was already beginning to coat the round stones in the bottom of the river. Another few days of these low temperatures and the Shyok would certainly freeze completely, but not soon enough for us. We sat down on the river flat and removed our shoes and socks and marched towards the rushing clear ribbon of water.

The pain was excruciating. It was about twenty below as I followed Skip across the shelf of ice that bordered the river, my skinny white feet radiating much of my body heat to the frigid air and the slick ice underfoot. Stepping off the ice into the knee-deep water my right foot found the slushy ice of the river-bed which moved around it like thick mud. As I moved cautiously forward the streaming water leeched all the remaining warmth from my feet, and I could no longer sense where my feet stopped and the ice began.

Using a ski pole to aid my balance I stumbled across the ice-shelf on the far side, threw down my pack and sat heavily upon it. The bitterly cold air attacked the wooden stumps that were my feet as I rubbed them with some gloves and pulled on my socks. Exclamations of various kinds were coming from the river as the others made their crossing and Skip, who had already put his shoes back on, was jumping up and down to aid circulation.

My pack on my back, the shoulder-straps seated snugly in the grooves cut there by the past two weeks of load-carrying, I walked on, leaving the group of groaning comrades by the river.

Eventually we reached the Chong Kumdan Glacier that spilled out of its side valley and sprawled across the narrows of the Shyok Gorge. Following the snout, we slithered across sections of moraine-covered ice and on to a narrow stretch of gravel. Even as we trekked along, the rising river surged higher on to the gravel platform, making us leap on to more elevated stretches of the shore. A constant jingle filled the air as drifts of last night's freeze broke loose and were swept downriver to collide with other sheets of ice adorned with giant crystals and create a cacophony of creaks and grating sounds.

A 2000-foot striated bluff stood opposite and it was easy to see how the glacier had driven across the river and into this great wall, creating an ice-dam that had banked up the water behind it.

'Look up there,' Skip said. 'You can see the old water mark up on the mountainside. That would have made the glacial lake at least five hundred feet deep.'

A pale line was drawn across the flank of the west side of the valley above the glacier. It was good evidence for the stories we had been told of the great ice-dam and the havoc it had caused down in the Indus Valley when the water had broken through the glacial dam.

Below the protrusion of the Chong Kumdan Glacier the valley issued on to a vast alluvial plain into which the river had cut a meandering groove. We were a sparsely threaded string of black beads tossed down upon the brown of the expansive valley floor and for every step we took the ones ahead seemed to multiply. Overlooking the river we stopped to rest our tired bodies.

'There're some horses coming!'

'I hope they're for us,' moaned Brett. His knee was very painful and it had swollen up overnight. To make matters worse his gym shoes were exploding at the seams.

Across the river we watched the line of horses come into view from behind a ridge that plummeted to the valley floor from a head of cloud. As they drew closer we could see that they were already carrying loads. We watched them cross the river below and wind their way up the bank towards where we sat. One of the men was an officer. That was evidenced by the fact that he rode a horse, as an officer should, I suppose, and by his rather plump and unfit appearance. A lot of mother's love had gone into his conditioning.

'Excuse me,' called Terry to the officer. He was about to ride past as if he had not seen us, which seemed peculiar as, apart from ourselves, there could have been no other distractions for several days' walk either way.

'Yes?' He seemed startled to be addressed, but halted his horse and turned to face Terry.

'Have you seen an expedition party near Saser Brangsa?'

'A party of an expedition. I have not seen this,' he replied.

'We are expecting to see them at Saser Brangsa. Do you know if there are any ponies coming up-valley for us?'

He did not know much about anything that we wanted to know. He was the new doctor for the Gepshan camp and was on his way to take up his post for the winter. He smiled sweetly, giving his horse a gentle kick with his heels, and continued after his caravan.

'They've gone on without us,' grumbled Brett. He seemed to complete each agonising sector of our trek fuelled by his venomous thoughts of Magan. He had never been so vociferous, being a man of few words. All of a sudden, here he was threading rows of stinging monosyllables together and showing an aptitude for it that belied his former reticence.

Down-valley we could see the jagged white spine of the Kichik Kumdan Glacier and since we had reconnoitred the route up there from Saser Brangsa we knew that with some effort we would make the distance to the flying-fox cable-way by evening. Skip and I moved off briskly, indulging our appetites in a fantasy luncheon of whatever our imaginations could muster as we went.

'Avocado and pink salmon . . .'

'Cottage cheese, lettuce and tomato . . .'

'Green broccoli . . .'

'Walnuts – and mustard!'

'Banana milkshakes . . .'

'Apricot crêpes . . .'

We rested at the Kichik Kumdan Glacier and before we resumed the trek we visited the narrow gut whose cataclysm of foaming monsoon water had so astonished us during our August reconnaissance. There had been a complete transition. The intimidating runnel from which no man would emerge alive was now quite benign. Blue waters swirled slowly around the immense boulders and sluggish eddies drifted with the current in the open runnel.

We crossed another large alluvial flat and skirted around the snout of the Au Tash Glacier, taking a low route for the last few miles in that head-down posture of the weary porter.

They had gone on.

We had reached the cable-way that stretched across the Shyok and we were greeted by emptiness. No messages and no evidence of their having stayed there. Our only hope was that our pony caravan was up near the military camp beneath the Saser La. Dave lit the stove and made some tea which we drank in a despondent silence. It was nearly dark when we heard Roddy, PV, Terry and Brett outside. They were not alone.

A pair of khaki trouser-legs and a sten-gun butt stepped into the frame of vision of the open tent door.

'How are you, mates?' came Terry's voice. 'We've been given some help by these army guys. Had a little lunch with them and they took most of our loads on their ponies.'

'Really! You lucky bastards.'

'PV and I will go on to the army camp and try to find the others,' said Roddy, poking his head into the tent.

They set off up the track while Brett and Terry crawled into the tent where Dave handed them cups of tea from a blackened billy. A candle flickered, throwing a pale yellow light on to our gaunt faces, and all I could think of was Madame Tussauds.

It was about nine o'clock when we heard the tramp of people approaching the tent. Looking out we saw two torch beams moving erratically in the blackness and before long were welcoming Roddy and Jonga into the tent. Never before had we been so pleased to see Jonga nor his huge pressure cooker which he had brought with him. The food was already prepared and it was the same old stuff. A congealed mixture of rice, sauces so hot that they threatened to blow the top off your head, and a yellow paste that he maintained was an edible form of lentil soup. But we were soon spooning it up.

'The others are camped just below the army,' Roddy informed us, 'and PV has stayed up there with them. They'll send some ponies down to help us early tomorrow morning. Meanwhile, there are a few things you should all know.'

Various sources had told Roddy that PV had searched our tents while we were at Base Camp. He had counted all our film and, it seems, read our journals and letters. Our outgoing letters had all been censored by the army and we had received only a small proportion of the incoming mail we should have. PV had also sent a letter to the commanding officer at Saser Brangsa telling him that Rajiv and Shashank were unpatriotic and sympathetic to foreigners and suggesting, predictably, that Jack was a CIA agent. This message had been responsible for their arrest and being marched at gun-point for three days over the Saser La to Sasoma for interrogation. What was more, Roddy told us, Magan had intended to continue without waiting for us but had been ordered to wait one more day by Prem who was in radio contact from Sasoma. Magan had done so, but was determined to leave the next morning very early, a decision that would again put us behind them. PV responded strongly to this and threatened to detain Magan by force until we were reunited.

As we had been told, Tenzing Dorje was at Saser Brangsa with a large number of ponies, but unwilling to assist us or to return to Base Camp to gather up our abandoned equipment, despite the fact he had been there for ten days living off our emergency food supplies. He intended to return to Sasoma the following day with us.

Four ponies filed down the mountainside to our camp and escorted us up to Saser Brangsa where the caravan group were dissembling their tents.

'Why didn't you wait for us, mate?' Terry barked.

'I have no need to wait for you,' snapped Magan and stormed off up the hill to the military camp.

'Where's that Tenzing Dorje?' Terry demanded next, looking around him.

As if on cue Tenzing Dorje walked up to the cook tent about which we were gathered.

'What's the story with the ponies?'

'It is not my fault, Terry. They did not want to go.'

'Then why have you stayed here for so long? Why didn't you go back to Sasoma?'

'I was waiting here for you.'

'You were asked to bring the ponies back to Base Camp. Why did you not do it? You are the man responsible for organising the ponies and you are the one who is supposed to see that the arrangements are carried out.'

It was mid-day before we left Saser Brangsa for the Saser La. Descending from the bone-littered pass we reached Sky-angpoche where we had to wait two hours for the ponies to arrive. It was bitterly cold and we broke up into groups to huddle together in the lee of boulders or within the walls of enclosures built by Ladakhi shepherds who had wisely returned to the relative lowlands of the Nubra Valley. I heard a furore over where one group was snuggled and decided that I would investigate, as much for curiosity as for the need to aid my circulation with a little movement. Wangchuk clutched the neck of an empty bottle of army rum. He was babbling to himself in a mixture of fluent Ladakhi, Hindi and stammered English, his multilingual nonsense interspersed with wild fits of hysterical giggling to which the huddle of bodies nearby responded with calls of encouragement.

'Have a drink, mate.'

Smash! Glass showered from the crest of a rock to testify to the current shortage of alcoholic refreshments in the Umlung Nala. Wangchuk shrieked with certifiable laughter, throwing his hands about as he did so, and then fell over backwards.

Next morning Magan, Errol and Wangchuk departed early for Sasoma. They planned to reach there in one day by going lightly laden and we hoped that they would be able to organise a truck to take us on to Leh. Time was running out as it was 14 October and our permit would expire the following day, the 15th.

We continued down-valley, the terrain gently falling away before us and, I suppose, we should have found the trekking easy had it not been for the weeks that had preceded it. I accompanied PV for several miles and we talked about his home in the prickly heat of southern India. I asked him why he had joined the army, which gave rise to a monologue of patriotism, the equal of which I have never heard before, nor wish to again. People who believe things with such fervour are dangerous.

We walked on in silence and eventually reached the abandoned army camp where we happily dropped our loads and slumped against the black-sooted walls of one of the shelters. An hour later the ponies arrived and we settled into the military ghost town for the night.

Next morning Skip and I descended the switchbacks to the Nubra where we were met by Magan, Errol and Wangchuk who greeted us with a muddle of news about the possibility of a truck to take us to Leh. The ponies began to arrive and with them our *bête noire*, Tenzing Dorje, evidently expecting nothing but gratitude from us on arriving at Sasoma and the long trek's end.

'Right, you bastard!' Terry had Tenzing by the scruff of the neck and was threatening him with his clenched fist. 'You didn't send us the ponies you said you would and you lied and cheated.'

'Why have you waited until the work is finished?' snapped Tenzing.

You haven't even done any work! You went to Tibet for a holiday.' Terry shoved him backwards and turned and marched away, as Dorje arrived with cups of tea and biscuits. Well timed, I thought to myself.

Two trucks rattled up. We tossed our gear on board and were soon on our way, jolting over the hummocks and hollows of the road which rumbled across the broad stretches of alluvial nothingness that separated villages, and eventually reached Panamik. We halted here to visit Stopdan and to see something of his village.

The pebble paths were flanked by irrigation ditches and the villagers had built adobe walls around their fields and to create privacy within their courtyards. Autumn leaves clung to the willows and poplars that fringed the fields and lined the maze of paths. The word was out that there were some odd-looking white people in town and smiling faces appeared over the tops of the walls to get prime-time viewing of the spectacle. Many of us were unquestionably pictures of dishevelment. My hair was matted like a Sadhu's, my jacket was ripped and stained with the dirt and use of two un-washed months and my gloves were little more than tatters; I filled the bill for Fagin in *Oliver Twist*, no further costume required.

Stopdan led us off the main path, past a gilded prayer-wheel that rang a dozen bells when we turned it, and through the tranquil lanes of Panamik. A large flag of grey stone bridged an irrigation canal on one side of the track and at its far end was a heavy wooden doorway. Stopdan pushed it open and, stepping into the courtyard beyond, called to his wife who appeared on a landing above us with a small child. She beckoned us to climb a ladder to the landing and ushered us into a room, on three sides of which was a low platform covered in carpets. In front of these were small tables. The walls were festooned with memorabilia and photographs of Stopdan in uniform as a highly decorated soldier in the Ladakh Scouts. There was a Buddhist shrine, with the Dalai Lama's picture alongside paintings of the Buddha and before them were silver butter lamps and incense.

While a huddle of spectators gathered at the door, Stopdan and his wife slapped glasses down on the tables in front of us and then splashed an opaque chung into them. It could have been the lack of exposure to alcohol in the past two months, but the first glass limbered everyone up, and cer-tainly contributed to the relaxation of that evening's journey down the Nubra Valley.

Four of us sat on the roof of the truck as it navigated the rough roads, forded streams and diverted around major wash-outs and culverts. As we passed through the villages we were greeted by crowds waving hands and calling 'Jullay, jullay'. Overhead the stars penetrated the deepening blue of the sky until they sparkled in the darkness of our mobile night.

Some hours later we reached Kalsa, a military transport station, where we were allowed to camp for the night. Women, particularly white ones, were a novelty here and some of the soldiers found their presence overwhelming.

'I will help you put this tent up,' said one slender fellow who could not stop grinning at Renée.

'No thank you,' intervened Dave. 'I have done it once or twice before. We can do it ourselves.'

'No, no. I insist.'

'Please, we would rather do it ourselves!'

'No, no. It is my duty. I must help you,' the soldier continued, and without taking his eyes off Renée he ran around trying to assist until the tent was in such confusion that Dave decided to set the chap straight. He drew himself up in front of him. 'I don't want you to help us. Go and help them.' He pointed to Skip and me. But the soldier obviously didn't find us as attractive as Renée.

We were kindly given dinner in the mess by the soldiers. The kerosene stove used both for cooking and for heating was, in Roddy's opinion, one of the most dangerous devices he had ever seen in the realm of kitchen equipment. A nozzle spurted raw fuel into the furnace which burned furiously with leaping yellow flames that drew one's attention to the leaking kerosene around the tank. We ate hastily, thanked the cooks with their oil-smeared faces and blackened hands and fled from the mess building. A little later we were all prostrate in our bags beneath a black and fateful sky.

Next morning we all crammed into one green canvas-topped truck that PV had arranged to take us to the Khardung La, 8000 feet above. The truck laboured slowly up the winding mountain road, spending most of its time in first gear. Clouds filled the sky and as we ascended the valley we disappeared into a world of mists, limited vision and lightly falling snow.

Suddenly the rear of the truck fish-tailed to the outside of the narrow road where the bank fell away for thousands of feet. The wheels had lost traction and spun, causing the snow to compact under the tyres and become a slick hollow of ice. The truck stopped and a dozen bodies ejected themselves from it in unison. The road was covered in a blanket of snow into which we sank and I became aware of how steep it was ahead. We all elected to walk.

Not far below the Khardung La and several miles to the north-west of it our truck was still ploughing on in first gear with clouds of black diesel billowing from the exhaust. We could see that the road cut left across some precipitous gullies to the obvious notch of the pass and I looked for the bridge that crossed the small glacier.

'Down there,' said Terry, pointing down the great mountainside to a twisted geometric object.

While the truck returned down-valley we began the thankless task of carrying our equipment along the avalanche-obstructed road towards the pass. Most of us hauled gear as well as the thirty kilos we carried on our backs. It was hard, breathless work as we slogged our way along the narrow remnants of the road, plugging steps through the waist-deep avalanche debris.

Halfway to the pass I reached a partially completed bridge which was now substantially under snow. It had no boards on it so we had to sidle along the inside of the structure between the glacial ice and the frame. Our obscene loads made this a desperate struggle and my skis kept catching on the underside of the bridge and sweeping fresh snow on to me off the girders. I followed the road round a bend and, before me, roared an avalanche. What had been clear road was suddenly deluged by a torrent of falling snow and when silence returned to the mountainside the road ahead had disappeared. I waded into the bright white candyfloss that barred the way and found myself sinking above my waist. The system that worked for me was falling forward, and here the weight of my pack helped, creating a huge hole into which I could then step.

There were more avalanches, about a dozen in all, which had to be traversed before the road turned south and on to the Khardung La. It was starting to snow and the wind drove the snowflakes into our faces with a stinging vengeance. I took my load to the temple and the road construction hut at the pass and left it outside before returning for another back-breaking carry.

At our gear dump I met PV who was just setting off with a particularly slim day-pack on his back, so I asked him if he could help by carrying one of the oars for our rafts with him as well.

'I am carrying the lieutenant's kit. This is not my own equipments,' he explained righteously. A young lieutenant had joined us in the truck up from Kalsa.

'That's okay, but what about helping us all by carrying a little more?' He looked astonished at this request. 'Look, you bastard, I'm not going to be your bloody coolie!' I shouted angrily. Before the words were out of my mouth I knew I had said something to which PV would be bound to respond. But in my wildest imaginings and in two months of enforced PV-watching I could never have anticipated such a reaction.

His eyes bulged out on stalks and his face went that dreaded puce colour. 'I am an Indian Army officer,' he roared, his voice breaking periodically. 'I am an officer. Are you threatening me! Yes, you are threatening me.'

'No, I'm not, PV. I am asking you to help us all by carrying more gear. I am sorry that I got annoyed. I still think that it would be good if you could carry some more gear.'

'I am enough for three men!' he screamed hysterically. 'Do you want to fight me?'

'No, PV. No, I don't. I am not a fighting man. You are the military man here, not me.'

'That's right,' he screamed. He was unreachable. Never have I seen a man do his block the way he was. It was all so absurd. Standing there on a high mountain pass at 18,000 feet, up to our knees in snow, shouting at one another. Was it the altitude, or the fatigue? It could have been Jonga's cooking but, most likely, it was the burgeoning tensions that had been growing for weeks.

'You son of a bitch!' he yelled.

'Stop screaming,' I yelled back.

'I can scream,' he roared back at me, then turned and stormed off.

I began sorting gear for my next ferry and had nearly completed packing the load and tying a haul rope to the barrel that I would drag behind me when Skip arrived, followed by the others.

'What happened with PV?'

'I asked him to carry a larger load. I shouted that I wasn't going to do all the work and he went crazy.'

'You can say that again, fella. He's promising to shoot us all and Magan is all heated up too.'

Then Terry marched into the conversation. 'You've gone too far, Peter. What happened with PV? He says he is going to get a gun from one of the soldiers.'

Before I could open my mouth, Magan had stormed up. 'Take off your pack, Peter. I am going to fight you. You have insulted an officer, you have insulted India. I am going to kill you.'

Suiting actions roughly to words, he began to charge me, flailing his fists in the air like a DC3 on take-off. Terry leapt between us, an action he later admitted could have been ill-judged, and planted a hand against Magan's chest in an effort to restrain him. It was all he needed for he stood there in front of Terry roaring at me and punching the air in gestures of aggression.

'I'll talk to PV,' I called back as I tramped away across the snow.

We had billeted ourselves in the road construction workers' hut and I approached it now with some apprehension. The thought of a trigger-happy PV at a window was distinctly unnerving. If I saw him I planned to drop to the ground and crawl to the side of the road where I would be able to find cover. The snow stung my eyes as I squinted through the blizzard conditions at the corrugated tin hut, from where there came no movement, no sound. I trod carefully, hoping to reach the door undetected.

I kicked the door open and stumbled in with the blizzard swirling about me. Miriam was tending a stove that flickered as she adjusted the jet.

'Where's PV?' I asked her.

She whispered, 'He's in there.' She looked down and continued what she was doing. She was as frightened as I was. I stepped up to the closed door of a small side room, knocked and pushed it open.

PV stood with his back to me. Errol was with him and he looked apprehensive.

'PV, can I have a word with you?'

He turned slowly. His eyes were still bloodshot and his facial muscles twitched with tension as he clenched his teeth.

'You are nothing!' he roared as he launched back into the same tirade he had begun on the mountainside. This time it lasted for a quarter of an hour.

'I am enough for three men. I am an officer. You cannot treat me like that. I will treat you like a jawan if I choose.'

Then to my horror he stepped across some ice-covered boards and rolled his pack over with his boot, exposing the evil, black and steely form of a sten gun. I froze. He slung the shoulder-strap over his arm and pointed the short sinister barrel with its perforated casing at my belly. He stood just two yards from me.

'Don't you worry,' he hissed melodramatically, 'it is loaded.' Then he proceeded with a succession of personal observations about my character. At the end of each outburst he demanded that I agree with him. I agreed with everything he said: after all, he had the gun.

'You are a disgrace to your father. He is the great man but he does not have the great son. You are the son of a bitch. You will be banned from India.' He heaved with excitement and lack of breath and I watched his grip tense on the sten. I didn't move. I only nodded and made affirmations regarding the astuteness of the way he was sizing me up.

'I will take you outside and bury you here. This is not Leh, this is not Delhi, this is army country. I can do this! I will bury you here.' He pointed with the barrel to the door. His voice cracked as he shrieked at me, regardless of pleas to stop from Errol. Eventually he sat down and lowered the gun.

I sighed with relief. I had never been threatened with a gun before and knew that I never wanted to be again.

'I will not help you or any of you. I forbid you to use the army trucks. I have the power to make the trouble for you. I can arrest you. I am an officer!'

'Yes, I know, PV.' I looked at him as he sat on the bed in the small side room, cradling the sten gun in his lap. His face was puffed and puce and the whites of his protruding eyes were red.

It was some time before the others made a strategic return from the gear dump. Roddy told me that they had listened for gun-fire and that he, personally, had expected to hear some.

'There were times when I did too,' I mumbled. I was really quite shocked by the whole ordeal and more than ever wanted our Karakoram journey to release its grips on us and set us free.

I needed some fresh air and some time to myself, so I returned to the wind and falling snow of the Khardung La and followed the diminishing ledge of the road back to the gear dump. Our tracks were disappearing under fresh snow and further avalanches. However, I was comforted by these wild elements and the opportunity to hurl myself into some hard physical work which helped numb the anguish that I felt inside. It was dark when I returned to the subdued atmosphere of the corrugated iron hut with the sixty-five kilos of equipment I had hauled through the storm.

Stopdan had given us a chicken when we were in Panamik and it was on the turbulent Khardung La that it met its maker and contributed to Jonga's final and redemptive act. He cooked an evening meal that was not only edible but almost palatable.

We returned outside to ferry loads from the dump. Errol helped us on one of these carries but Magan and PV remained by the oil heater where they maintained a stately isolation from the workers. It was nearly mid-day before the first truck arrived up the snow-drifted road from South Pulu and Leh. It was filled with men and women who worked for the army's road construction company. They were a cheery lot and talked incessantly as they cleared the snow from the bridge and continued to assemble the new structure.

The major in charge of the bridge reconstruction was an affable and accessible fellow. Armed with only a heavily waxed and curled moustache, he spent several hours with Magan and PV and eventually succeeded in making them see some reason and allow us to join the roadworkers in the truck for the journey down to Leh.

The wind blew and it was snowing again. There was one truck and two jeeps and about seventy people, plus our truckload of gear. Twelve soldiers commandeered one of the jeeps and the major gallantly invited Miriam and Renée to join him in his, leaving a noisy rabble of fifty-five to attempt to squeeze into the truck.

I would have called it a bull rush, had it not been for the large contingent of Ladakhi women who constituted the most forceful and vociferous subgroup among us, as everyone simultaneously attempted to board the truck with their gear. Asphyxiation seemed a possibility and being crushed even more likely. One man beside me spent most of the time completely submerged by bodies with only his head visible, and a young monk from the Nubra Valley found the rocking of the truck and pressing bodies too much for his youthful constitution. He dribbled and vomited over us all for the six hours of the journey to Leh.

At South Pulu I climbed on to the roof and rode upon the bucking-bronco canopy of the truck down the steep switchbacks below South Pulu and into Leh, passing through the police checkpost without stopping, which was probably just as well as we were now a day overdue for our Inner Line permit.

We spent two days in Leh. Everyone washed and appeared in fresh clothes and Brett and Roddy shaved off their beards. They were barely recognisable, looking as if they had regained their youth.

We had hoped to be able to fly direct to Delhi but tickets were impossible to get as a new airport terminal was to be opened and the airline was flying in a planeload of dignitaries for the ceremony, which increased the waiting list by a hundred. We were told that the first available confirmed seats would be in early November. There was no choice but to charter a bus for the hectic drive to Srinagar in Kashmir.

A bus backed into the hotel car-park and we began the job of loading our baggage for our forty-eight hour drive to Srinagar. It was mid-day and I noticed Terry had a worried look upon his face, so I assumed that another obstacle had arisen.

'The driver says the Zoji La is blocked.' The Zoji La is the critical mountain pass on the road between Leh and Srinagar.

'Oh, good!' I said, slipping into a delirium of sarcasm. 'I am so happy.'

An hour later we were seated in the bus and bound for the Zoji La if not Srinagar. I don't think any of us thought we would ever reach New Delhi, in under a month anyway. However, we were determined to give it a try.

The seats were as hard as splintered boards and the suspension non-existent. I picked up a spectacular bout of giardia that had me vomiting like a geyser and suffering the most humiliating diarrhoea. The road wound its way through the beautiful moonscapes of Ladakh and passed through a succession of villages lined with the bright autumn yellow of poplars. We followed the hair-raising switchbacks that traced their way through the Indus Gorge, massive purple hillsides stretching above us adorned with a curious weave of colour and texture. Beneath the road flowed the turquoise ribbon of the river as it cut its way through the decaying topographic chaos of the Ladakh mountains.

Among the passengers and drivers of the 150 trucks and buses parked in disarray around the checkpost at Drass there was a rumour circulating that a truck had rolled over on the pass. The road had already been closed for four days. No one was allowed through, a soldier told Errol, until an army convoy had arrived from Srinagar and that, he said, could take a long time.

'We started with many adventures on this expedition,' said Magan philosophically, 'and now it looks as if we shall finish with many also.' He looked across at the checkpost, his face a picture of forlorn resignation.

We waited all day at the checkpost until, late in the afternoon, the army trucks started to roll through. There were hundreds of them and they kept coming for several hours: an endless mechanical millipede making for the barren hills to the north. Finally, a military jeep passed with a flag flying from its roof. This was the end of the army convoy.

A tall soldier with 'MP' displayed on his arm stood by the checkpost barrier. He raised a shiny whistle to his lips and blew one long, shrill blast. Suddenly, we were engulfed in a Grand Prix start as every engine billowed black exhaust and passengers scrambled for their seats. The trucks and buses barged into the funnel of the open barrier and charged out on to the road, parping their horns in a frenzy of excitement. It was five in the evening and we were on our way to Srinagar.

A wave of vehicles trailed into the mountains and through the snow, many of the drivers steering with reckless abandon. One of the roadsigns warned, 'Follow my curves smoothly', a message that seemed unlikely to keep the drivers' minds on the road. Survival dominated our thoughts as our ancient bus hiked on to the intimidating Zoji La. The road was etched across a great mountain flank with precipices plunging several thousand feet to the river that foamed in the dark gorge below. Soon we were negotiating this lethal road in the pitch black of the night, a queue of glowing headlamps suspended during the remarkable eclipse of the crossing. We had left the aridity of Central Asia and had returned to the scented forests of more familiar terrain.

We were all relieved to descend to the legendary vale of Kashmir but in Srinagar there were still no air tickets available for three weeks. We should have to take another bus for the long journey through the Himalaya down to the plains. But for that night we were happy to settle into comfortable beds on a houseboat in Srinagar.

I awoke to luxury. Cedar-panelled walls and vaulted ceiling enclosed the spacious room which swayed in the wake of a passing motorboat. Finely woven carpets covered the floors and ornately carved furniture filled the rooms and lounges and the dining hall of our cultural metamorphosis. I rolled out of the unaccustomed comfort of the large bed, dressed and strolled out on to the verandah with its intricate trellis and views across the tranquillity of the lake. Beneath my feet I felt the gentle pitching of the houseboat as I soaked up warmth from the sun, closed my eyes and stood listening to some words that kept revolving in my head:

> For all experience is an arch
> Wherethrough gleams that untravelled world
> Whose margins fade forever
> And ever when I move.

Epilogue

For some of the expedition members there have been major changes in their lives since we all parted.

It was probably just as well that Prem did leave us early, for when he returned home he found that his son was seriously ill and was able to be by his side at the New Delhi hospital while the child was convalescing. Prem eventually returned to Manali and continues to direct the Mountaineering Institute there. JP went back to his engineering work, Shashank to the travel industry and Magan to the deserts of Rajastan, although he, true to his word, has returned to the mountains for other expeditions. Rajiv wedded Jyoti in the city of Jammu on 22 October 1986, and a year later Errol was married too. Commander Jogindar Singh continues his involvement with the Indian Mountaineering Foundation and has taken up a post with Vayadut Airlines in New Delhi after many years with Air India. Wangchuk continues his work with trekking and rafting in Ladakh and no one has heard from PV.

Dave and Renée returned to Sydney where they had a baby daughter and Dave is working as a draughtsman. Terry continues to spend most of his time in the Himalaya where he works for World Expeditions as a trekking guide and Brett has reluctantly gone back to work as an electrician. Skip periodically sends me cards from different parts of the world wherever his work as a raftsman with Sobek takes him, and Roddy went back to farming in Victoria's western districts, although he has made several trips to India to further the cause of the heliski operation that a number of us have been involved in near Manali. Miriam went back to the bank in Sydney and I returned to Melbourne where I married Ann, bought a house in the city, with flower boxes and a park across the street, and spend my leisure hours wondering what next to do – this has not proved to be an insurmountable problem.